Miranda Tufnell is a dancer and choreographer. She trained at the London School of Contemporary Dance and at the Cunningham Studio New York. Returning from the United States in the mid-70s she became an early member of Rosemary Butcher's dance group, but since 1976 she has choreographed and performed her own work – often in art galleries, making extensive use of light and sound environments; and with Chris Crickmay, she made a film, *Dance Without Steps*, for the Open University. Her work has also involved a long-standing collaboration with the dancer Dennis Greenwood. *Landlight*, her most recent work, was performed in London in 1989. Her work of the last fifteen years has been accompanied by periods of teaching. She lives in Cumbria.

Chris Crickmay has been involved over the past ten years researching the relationship of art to performance, and in improvisation and mixed media work in dance. Several of his articles have appeared in *Contact Quarterly*, and *New Dance* among others. *Field*, a work in movement and extended media, a collaboration with Mary Fulkerson, was performed in London, Norway and Denmark. He has a Bachelor of Architecture degree from Liverpool University, as well as a postgraduate diploma in Design Research from the University of Manchester, Institute of Science and Technology. He is now Head of the Department of Art and Design at Dartington College of Arts. He lives in Devon.

BODY
SPACE
IMAGE

Notes towards
improvisation and
performance

Miranda Tufnell
Chris Crickmay

DANCE BOOKS

First published 1990
This edition published 1993, reprinted 2001, 2006 by
Dance Books Ltd, The Old Bakery,
4 Lenten Street, Alton, Hampshire GU34 1HG

ISBN 1 85273 041 2

A CIP catalogue record for this title
is available from the British Library

Printed in Great Britain by Latimer Trend and Company Ltd,
Plymouth, Devon

CONTENTS

ACKNOWLEDGEMENTS

The ideas in this book are drawn from a body of work which has developed in the last thirty years, with roots that go back much further to the turn of the twentieth century. They include the work of Loie Fuller in the 1890s, Isadora Duncan from 1900, Futurist performance from 1910, early expressionist films, the Bauhaus from 1919, the theatre work of Artaud in the 1920s and 1930s, the collaborative work of John Cage and Merce Cunningham from 1944, Anna Halprin, Allan Kaprow, Tadeusz Kantor and others from the 1950s. It is a history in which independent developments coming from dance, visual art, music, poetry and theatre, with their separate origins, frequently became interwoven with each other and also drew inspiration from everyday activities and from other disciplines. Dance drew especially from other body disciplines, ancient (such as Tai Chi) and modern (such as Alexander Technique). Research into the relationship between movement and our mental images of our own anatomy, pioneered by Mabel Todd and others, have also continued to feature in improvised dance.

The attitudes to mind, body and environment which underlie improvisation are themselves ancient, perhaps a fundamental human stance, to be found today as a way of life in some aboriginal cultures.

The last thirty years of development in dance, the start of which was marked by the work of the Judson Group in the early 1960s, have provided us with our main sources, together with parallel developments in Performance Art and Visual Theatre, and we have deliberately mixed ideas from these different sources. We have found inspiration from the work and teaching of: Steve Paxton, Simone Forti, Mary Fulkerson, Nancy Topf, Eva Karczag, Remy Charlip, Don Burton, Joseph Beuys, Christopher Jones and many others.

We would like to express our thanks to Hugh Brody for sustained and detailed help with the text and to Eva Karczag, Huw Davies, Rick Allsopp, and Suzanne Lacy for advice at strategic moments.

We are indebted for substantial written contributions from Sylvia Hallet (on sound), Rose English, Jacky Lansley, Suzanne Lacy, Penny Saunders, Steve Paxton, Angela Carter, Caroline Tisdall, Kō Murobushi and to Lucy Lippard for permission to use part of a previously published article.

We would also like to thank Dave Kenyon for his work in preparing photographic prints.

For permission to use pictures of their work and/or contributing written commentaries, we would like to thank: Eiko and Koma, Rose English, Sankai Juku, Lizzy Slater, Steve Paxton, Eva Karczag, Nancy Stark Smith, Sue MacLennan, Simone Forti, Rosemary Butcher, Eleanor Antin, Mary Fulkerson, Jacky Lansley, Katy Duck, Gary Stevens, The Welfare State Company, John Davies, Anthony Howell, Rose Garrard, Forkbeard Fantasy, Kate Blackner, IOU Company, David Ward, Deborah Thomas, Tim Head, Alastair MacLennan, Bow Gamelan, Elizabeth Vellacott, Gaby Agis, Suzanne Lacy,

Sally Potter, Shirley Cameron and Roland Miller, Charlie Hooker, Trevor Wishart, David Medalla, Pina Bausch and the Trinbago Carnival Club.

In addition to photographs and quotations acknowledged in the text, grateful acknowledgement is made to the following for permission to reproduce material copyrighted or controlled by them:

Igaku-Shoin Ltd: The Bony Skeleton of the Entire Human Body Disassembled, pxiv; *Ribs*, p16, from *Photographic Anatomy of the Human Body* by C Yokochi and J W Rowan, 2nd Edition 1978. Harper and Row, Publishers, Inc, Vertebral Column, p8, and Principal Veins in Anterior View, p24, from *Principles of Anatomy and Physiology* by Gerard Tortora and Nicholas Anagnostakos, *c*.1984 by Biological Science Textbooks, Inc, and Elia-Sparta, Inc. Macmillan and Co Ltd: Lateral View of The Vertebral Column, p16; Superior View of The Male Pelvis, p15; The Surface Projection of The Trunk Skeleton, p17; the bones of the right hand, p33, from *Textbook of Human Anatomy* edited by W J Hamilton, 1958. Oxford University Press: Normal Sacrum, p15; Anteroposterior Bronchogram, p26, from *Cunningham Textbook of Anatomy* edited by G K Romans, 11th Edition 1972. Faber and Faber: The Skeleton, Anterior Aspect, p37, from *Anatomy of The Human Body* by Lockhart Hamilton and Fife, 1959. Lennart Nilsson: Human Brain and Nervous System, pp40 and 41, from *Behold Man* by Lennart Nilsson, published by Harrap, 1974. Harper and Row: quotation from *One Hundred Years of Solitude*, p115, by Gabriel Garcia Marquez. Jerome Rothenberg: Statement by Kábbo, African Bushman, p206, from *Technicians of the Sacred* edited by Jerome Rothenberg, Anchor Books, 1969. André Kertez, New York, Musée d'Art Moderne, Centre Georges Pompidou, Paris.

EVERY DAY
LIE RESTING

WHAT IS NEEDED
TO BE MORE COMFORTABLE

LET GO OF PAST AND FUTURE

OPEN THE ROOM OF YOURSELF
TO THE DAY OF THIS BREATH

OPEN THE SKIN TO THE AIR
TO THE LIGHT

LET THE UNDERSURFACES OF THE BODY
OPEN   INTO   SHADOWS

LET THE WHOLE BODY FILL
AND OPEN TO THE BREATH

STRETCH   ROLL   YAWN   DREAM

LET   THE   THOUGHTS   DISSOLVE   AND   SPREAD   THEMSELVES

EACH DAY FIND A NEW QUESTION

Sankai Juku, *Kinkan Shonen, The Cumquat Seed*, 1984
Photo Osamu Nojiri

INTRODUCTION

This book is about improvisation – exploring, looking and listening. We live in changing landscapes of movement, people, objects, spaces, light, sound, words and stories. Improvisation is a way of shifting the boundaries within which we experience our world.

In being receptive to the immediate moment and in tuning in to our own sensations, feelings, dreams, we begin our own narrative of discovery that differs from the received narratives of our culture.

Any creative process is to this extent improvised (involves states of not knowing what comes next). This book is concerned with improvisation as a source of creativity and as a way of opening imagination.

Improvisations require different styles of thought at different moments in their evolution. A dialogue is needed between wildness and order – between setting the mind loose and measuring objectively. The book reflects this in its changes of 'voice' between practical statement and image-based material intended to seed new thought and action. The text is accumulative, each section adding another dimension.

The book begins with the body and moves through to the settings or circumstances within which improvisation may develop. It is intended as a manual, an aid to action, but it is not in any sense a complete guide. It sets out to stimulate rather than instruct and each part should be understood as a series of starting points from which the reader will set out upon a journey.

1   MAPPING THE BODY

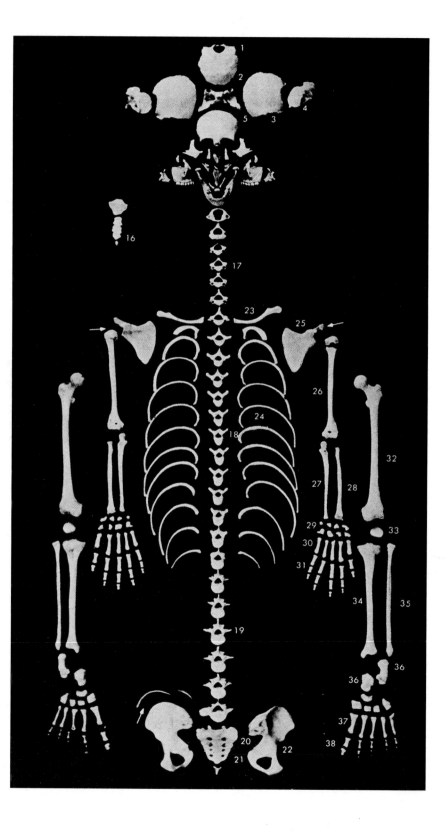

Our bodies are the reflections of our lives: sitting, walking, standing, we absorb the impact of each day. Each thought and sensation makes changes in the body. Daily preoccupations affect energy, posture and therefore mobility. This section is concerned with becoming 'present', attentive to the immediate moment in preparation for working. The state in which you begin work determines the quality of material found.

The text presents a series of mental images concerning the structure and function of the body – 'bone meditations'*. These images are intended to create a sense of openness – an availability for movement. These in combination with stillness and resting are a way of unloosing the body/mind from the ongoingness of our everyday habits of perception. The body, how it moves and dreams, becomes a route to the imagination.

Take an image, let it hang in the mind, let the sensation of the thought dissolve through the body. Let the movement inside of the body – of breath, of thoughts – move the outside. Allow the sensations their own time and expression – yawning, rolling, resting – waiting for a space between the thoughts, an unlocking of the parts of the body – a gap into which something new can emerge.

*A term derived from Remy Charlip

HEAD

IS FULL OF OPENINGS
WINDOWS FOR THE SENSES

openings of eye, ear, mouth, fontanelle,
in the jaw, under the eyes,
an opening at the base of the skull

LET THE EYES REST IN DEEP POOLS OF THE EYE SOCKETS
LET THE HEARING DEEPEN
SOFTEN THE TONGUE IN THE CAVE OF THE MOUTH

The head is made up of 29 bones. Eight bones form the cranium and 14 bones make up the face. Most of our interaction with the world is mediated by the head – hearing, seeing, balancing, smelling, breathing, eating.

Inside the protection of the skull floats the brain, which elongates into the spinal cord – flows down the spine, separates into the sciatic nerve at the sacrum and continues on down to the toes. A clear fluid, the cerebro-spinal fluid, is produced in the centre of the brain and bathes the spinal cord, pulsing down to the base of the spine and returning upwards 9 or 10 times a minute, a constant tide of connection between head and pelvis.

We tend to imagine the bones of the body as hard/inert, but all the bones, including the bones of the skull, are alive and changing. It is in the bones that the red blood cells are formed. The skeleton can renew itself over 20 months.

THE HEAD MOVES UP
THE BODY FOLLOWS

FEEL THE AIR AROUND THE BACK OF THE HEAD

LET THE BACK OF THE HEAD BE FULL
BALANCING THE FRONT OF THE FACE
LET THE JAW HANG EASY AS THE ARM

eight bones make up the back of the head
fourteen bones make up the front of the face

LET THE BONES OF THE SKULL SOFTEN
AND   MOVE   APART

LIGHT SHINES THROUGH

THE BONES OF THE SKULL MOVE
AS DO THE PLATES OF THE EARTH

LET THE SKULL HOLD THE BRAIN LIGHTLY

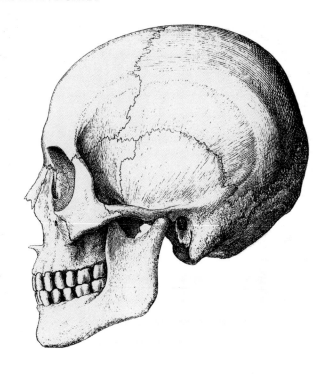

The head balances on the spine midway between the ears;
eyes, nose and organs of balance are situated
close to this meeting of head and spine.

BREATHE IN TO THE TIP OF THE SPINE

LET THE BREATH FILL THE INSIDE OF THE HEAD

SOFTENING THE BONES OF THE SKULL
BEHIND THE EYES, INSIDE THE JAW

THE HEAD ROUND AND SOFT

IMAGINE THE WHOLE HEAD
MALLEABLE TO THE BREATH

THE ROUNDNESS OF THE HEAD IS ECHOED
IN THE ROUNDNESS OF THE RIBCAGE,
OF THE PELVIS, OF THE HEELS,
OF THE ROOF OF THE MOUTH

SEE THE OPENING AT THE BASE OF THE SKULL
WHERE THE BRAIN ELONGATES
AND FLOWS DOWN
TO THE SACRUM

THE SACRUM MOVES DOWN
AS THE BACK OF THE HEAD FILLS
AND MOVES UP

THE HEAD LISTENS
TO THE BODY
THROUGH THE SPINE

Sankai Juku, *Outdoor Event*, 1984
Descending the walls of the old city of Jerusalem
hanging upside down from a rope.

ALLOW THE NECK TO LENGTHEN UPWARD
OUT OF THE ROUNDNESS OF THE RIBS
SUPPORTING THE HEAD HIGH IN THE AIR

SEE THE VIEW FROM THE TIP OF YOUR SPINE

OPEN ALL THE WINDOWS OF THE HEAD

THE PORES OF THE SKIN

THE HEAD TAKES THE WHOLE BODY ON A JOURNEY

THE WHOLE HEAD IS:

TOP   BACK   UNDERNEATH   SIDE   FRONT

OPENING   LISTENING

IN   ALL   DIRECTIONS

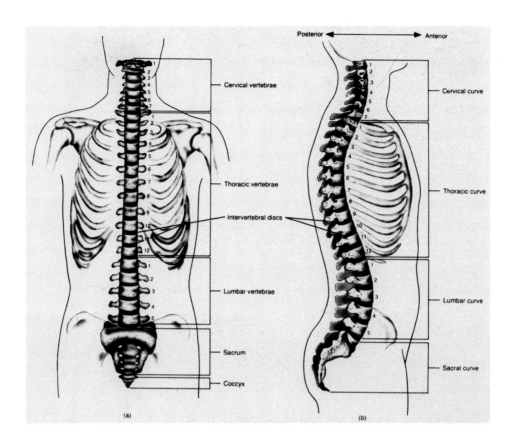

Vertebral column: anterior and right lateral view.

The spine is the power centre of the body, both a moving column of support connecting head, limbs, thorax and pelvis, and a protective corridor for the spinal cord. Alignment of the spine therefore affects the entire functioning of the body.

The spine is made up of 33–34 vertebrae.

7 cervical vertebrae make up the neck
12 thoracic from which the ribs extend
5 lumbar
5 fused sacral, which provide a stable base for the ascending stack of vertebrae
4–5 coccygeal, the remnant of the tail

The accumulated weight of head, thorax and limbs is transferred down the vertebral column to the pelvis, which acts as a bridge spreading the weight down through the legs and into the floor.

Between each of the vertebrae lie discs, spongy and fluid filled. These act as self-adjusting cushions between the vertebrae and protect the spinal nerves as they emerge from the cord. The discs make up a quarter of the total length of the spine, being proportionally larger in the more flexible areas of the spine. They form:

40% of the cervical
33% of the lumbar
20% of the thoracic
(there is no movement in the sacrum, which has no discs)

It is said that the spine is 2 inches longer in space than on the earth. The downward pull of gravity compresses the discs. Lying flat on the back it takes twenty minutes for the discs to reflate. Fixing or holding the rib cage and shoulders also interferes with the spine's length and flexibility.

The vertebrae vary in shape, but their basic form is the same: a cylindrical weight-bearing 'body' in front, with a vertical arch extending out from it through which the spinal cord passes. From the arch extend 7 processes or individual spines, to which the numerous ligaments and muscles controlling movement of the spine are attached. It is the tip of the main spinal process that can be felt as knobs lying down the back of the spine.

The front of the spine is much deeper in the body than usually realised. At the waist, half the body's volume is made up of the spine and its attached muscles.

THE SPINE IS A LONG LIMB

SPACING

        HEAD

        RIBCAGE

        PELVIS

FROM THE TIP OF THE COCCYX
UP TO THE BASE OF THE SKULL
BETWEEN THE EARS

A LONG SPINE FALLING UP

IN THE SPINE ONE CURVE
LEVERS ANOTHER
THE CURVE OF THE LUMBAR RISES
INTO THE CURVE OF THE THORAX

THE CURVE OF THE NECK
RISES UP
INTO THE HEAD

SEE THE CURVES OF THE SPINE

LENGTHENING

UPWARD   AND   DOWNWARD

ALLOW THE REST OF THE BODY TO BALANCE
AROUND A CURVING RIVER OF SPINE

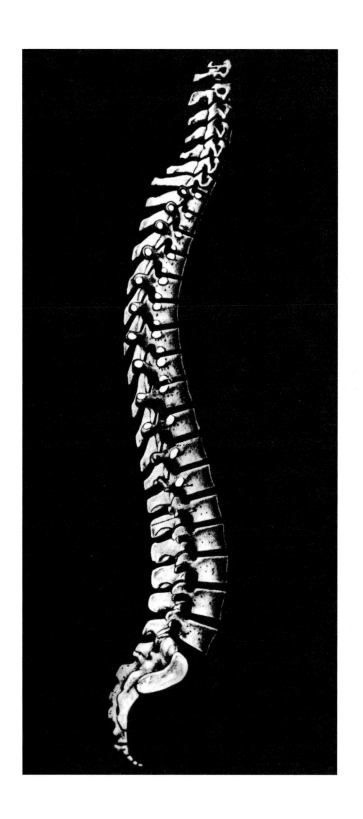

SEE THE DISCS AS CUSHIONS OF AIR

SPACING

ONE   VERTEBRA
FROM   ANOTHER

PLACE A CUSHION OF AIR
BETWEEN EACH OF THE VERTEBRAE
IN YOUR SPINE

LET EACH VERTEBRA FLOAT UP

FEEL THE SUPPORT OF THE EARTH
UP THROUGH THE CENTRE OF THE FEET, LEGS, THIGH SOCKETS
LET THE SUPPORT RISE THROUGH THE BODIES OF THE VERTEBRAE
UP TO THE BASE OF THE HEAD

SOFTEN DOWN THE OUTSIDE OF THE BODY

SEE THE SPINES OF THE VERTEBRAE AS HEELS
LIKE THE HEEL BONE OF THE FOOT
LET DOWN THE HEELS OF THE SPINE

UNROLL A TAPEMEASURE DOWN YOUR BACK
RIGHT TO THE HEELS OF THE FEET

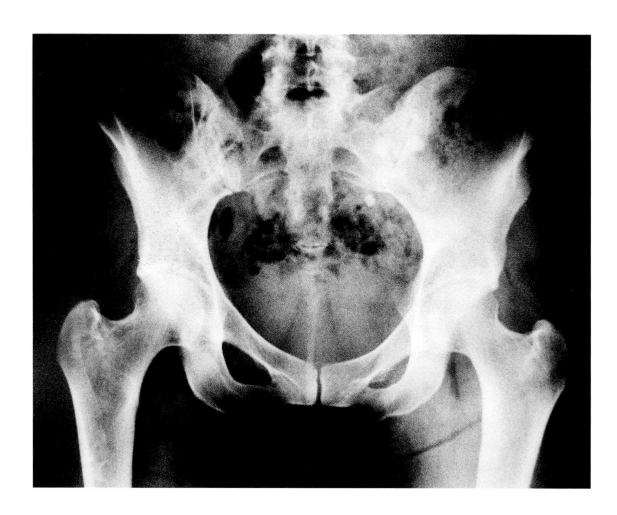

THE SACRUM IS MADE UP OF

5 FUSED BONES

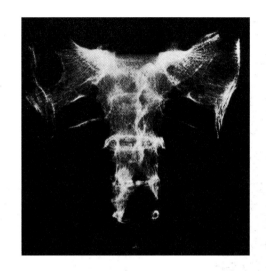

SEE THEM SEPARATE
AND   M O V E

DOWNWARDS

SEE THE WING BONES OF THE ILIUM AS EARS OPENING

TO ALLOW THE SACRUM TO SLIDE DOWN BETWEEN

LET THE HEAD MOVE UP AS THE SACRUM MOVES DOWN

UP   TO THE HEAVENS
DOWN   TO THE CENTRE OF THE EARTH

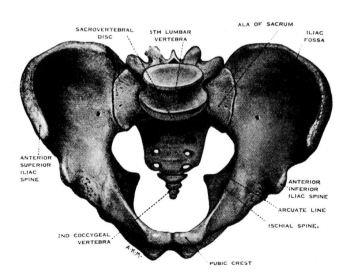

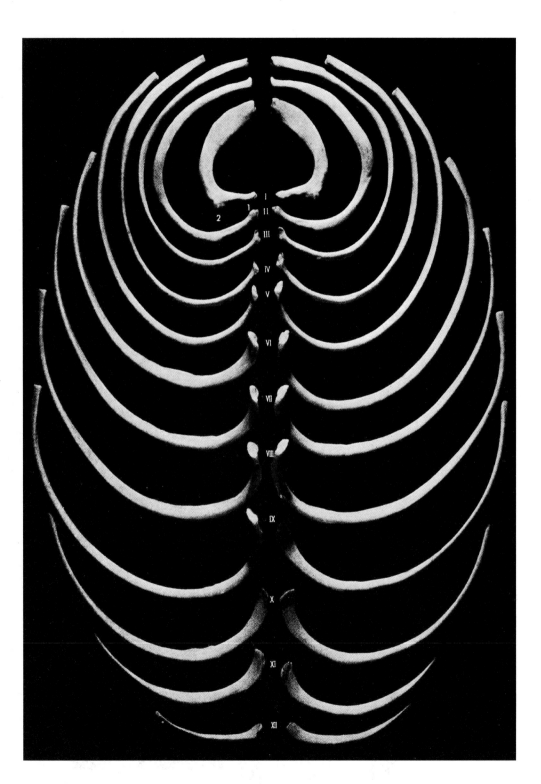

THE BACK IS WIDE

LET THE RIBS OPEN LIKE WINGS FROM THE SPINE

SEE THE RIBS AS ARMS
INTO WHICH YOU CAN REST

LET THE FRONT OF THE BODY SOFTEN
AND OPEN   FROM THE THROAT   TO THE PELVIS

LET SUPPORT COME FROM THE BACK

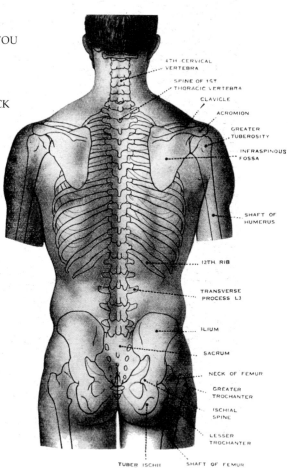

SEE YOUR OWN BACK   IN FRONT OF YOU

STEP FORWARD INTO YOUR OWN BACK

SEE IT BEHIND YOU   AND   STEP   BACK

SHADOWS

ECHOES

MOVING INTO THE SPACE
BEHIND YOU

Henri Matisse, *Acrobats*, 1952
© DACS 1989
© H. Matisse Estate 1990
Photo Archives (D.R.)

HEAD   RIBCAGE   PELVIS

LET THE SPINE TAKE THE HEAD FOR A RIDE

LET THE RIBS MOVE THE SPINE

LET THE SPINE BE THE ROOT FOR THE ARMS AND LEGS

A MOVING SPINE IN A MOVING BACK

THE RIGHT SIDE OF THE BODY KNOWS THE LEFT SIDE
THROUGH THE SPINE

A CONTINUOUS DIALOGUE

U P   A N D   D O W N

A N D   A C R O S S

Photo Ulli Stelzer

THE BREATH

FROM THE MOMENT OF BIRTH
TO THE MOMENT OF DEATH

THE BREATH FILLS AND EMPTIES THE BODY

OF ITS OWN ACCORD

TRAVELLING TO EACH CELL OF THE BODY

SEE THE BREATH AS LIGHT

SUN FILLING THE ROOM OF YOUR BODY

WATCHING THE BREATH

NOT CHANGING IT

How we breathe affects how we eat, talk, sleep, move, think. The breath is our fuel for life – a cell cannot survive more than a few minutes without air/oxygen.

The diaphragm is the muscle which initiates breathing; after the heart the most active muscle in the body. The diaphragm is a dome of muscle, 12–15 inches in diameter, which stretches across the torso, dividing thorax from abdomen. It is attached to the lower border of the ribs and anchored down into the lower back. It acts as a floor for the lungs and heart and a roof for the stomach and viscera.

The diaphragm functions much as a piston. On inhalation, the dome of the diaphragm contracts downwards. Air is drawn into the lungs. As the diaphragm relaxes back up, air is pressed out of the lungs.

The lungs hang in the upper ribcage, their largest portion lying towards the back of the torso. They are composed of millions of tiny air sacs, or alveoli, which hang like a forest of small grapes inside the top of the ribcage. Their surface area is c100 sq yards – 40 times greater than that of the skin. These alveoli are networked with a fine mesh of capillaries through which the blood passes.

Oxygen is drawn into the blood from the air sacs and carbon dioxide expelled. The newly aerated blood is then pumped to the billions of cells that make up the body. Full lung capacity varies from 7–40 litres of air per minute, depending on the degree of bodily exertion or rest.

The action of breathing – the movement of the diaphragm – increases the volume of the torso, creating movement in the spine and ribcage, and affects the rhythm of the digestion and heart. Allowing the movement of the breath helps dissolve tension, or holding, in the body; the breath is a useful barometer of our state of attention or tension.

Watching/allowing the rhythm of the breath helps the body find its own timing – the time of one step to another; between one word/thought, and the next; the timing of sleeping/waking.

We share the air in the room between us.

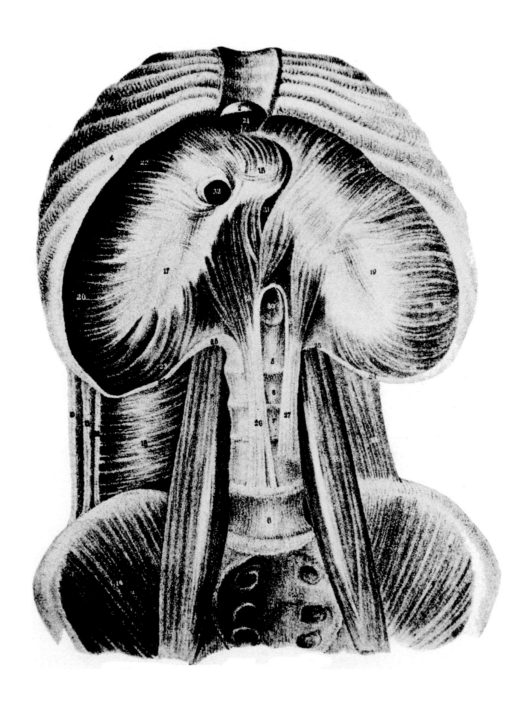

The diaphragm, showing muscular attachments
down to the lower spine and pelvis

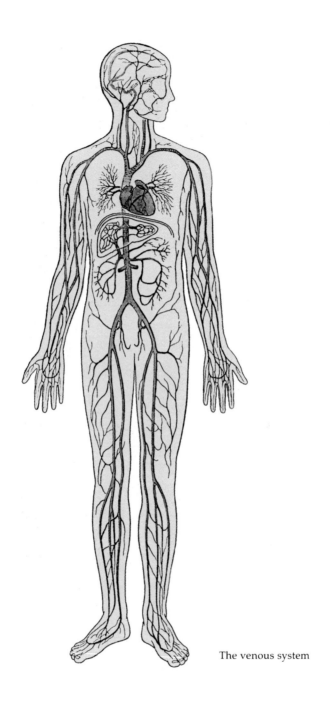

The venous system

The blood takes up oxygen from the lungs and
carries it around the body via a system of arteries.
The de-oxygenated blood returns to the lungs via
a corresponding system of veins.

BREATHE IN
FROM THE SOLES OF THE FEET

LET THE BREATH RISE UP
THROUGH THE INSIDE OF THE BODY

BREATHE OUT
THROUGH THE TOP OF THE HEAD

LET THE SKIN   ARMS   RIBS   LEGS
HANG LIKE BRANCHES
MOVING ON THE WIND OF YOUR BREATH

WALKING

IMAGINE THE BODY PERMEABLE TO AIR

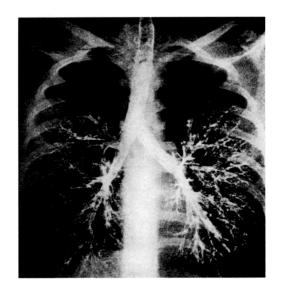

YAWNING

LET THE SOFT PALATE OPEN UPWARDS
INTO THE DOME OF THE HEAD

LET THE YAWNS OPEN THE INTERIOR SPACES OF THE BODY

THE BREATH IS THE MEANS BY WHICH THE INSIDE OF THE BODY
KNOWS THE OUTSIDE

LET THE AIR SUPPORT YOU LIKE WATER

LET   THE   BREATH   TRAVEL   DOWN

OPENING THE GATEWAYS
OF SHOULDERS
ELBOWS
WRISTS
KNEES
ANKLES

LET THE BREATH FILL YOU
TO YOUR FULL SIZE

ON THE OUT BREATH
LET GO

OF TIREDNESS

PAIN

WAITING

LET THE BREATH GIVE THE BODY

T I M E

YAWNING   LENGTHENING   STRETCHING   FOLDING   ROLLING

EACH BREATH A DIFFERENT STORY

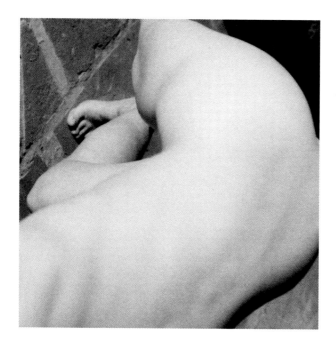

Photo Hugh Brody

THE ARM IS LONG

IMAGINE A LIQUID SPACE
IN EACH OF THE JOINTS
LONG ARMS FOLDING AND UNFOLDING
AT SHOULDERS / ELBOW / WRIST / FINGERS

THE ARM BRANCHES AT BOTH ENDS

IN   TO THE CENTRE OF THE BODY

OUT   TO THE TIPS OF THE FINGERS

IMAGINE A BRIGHTNESS
AT THE BREASTBONE
LET IT SHINE TO THE TIPS OF THE SHOULDERS

THE CLAVICLES ARE LONG AND CURVING

OPENING THE ARMS OUT
FROM THE CENTRE OF THE BODY

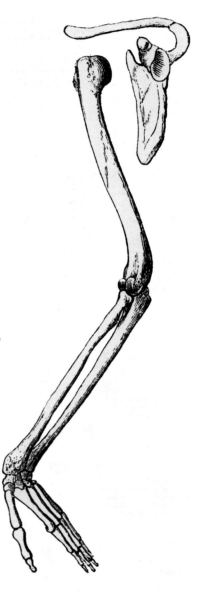

The arm fans out like the branch of a tree from the single bone of the humerus to the 26 bones of each hand.

The arm hangs from the shoulder girdle. This loosely linked 'yoke' – clavicles in front and scapulae in back – supports and at the same time anchors the arm into the torso.

The shoulder girdle floats free of the rib cage and is attached to the skeleton only at the sternum. This allows the right side to act independently of the left.

The clavicles are two long and curving bones that rest on the sternum just at the base of the throat. Their action is to open the arms out from the centre of the body so that the action of the arms – pushing, carrying, lifting – does not affect the vital functioning of heart, stomach and lungs.

The outer tips of the clavicles articulate with the scapulae from which the arms hang. A network of muscles connect the scapulae to the full length of the spine.

The tips of the lungs lie just behind the clavicles and the first ribs. The shoulder girdle rests on the rib cage which rises and falls with the breath.

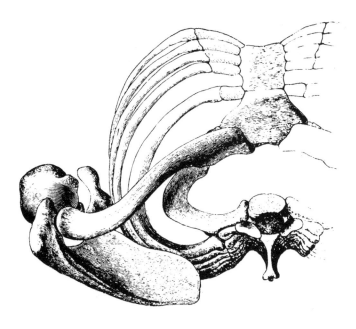

View of the shoulder girdle from above, scapulae at the back, clavicles at the front

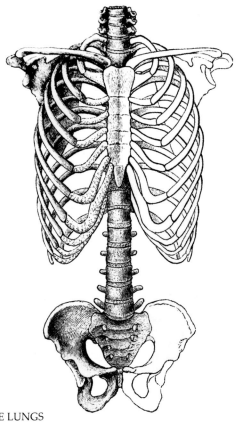

SEE THE RIBS CIRCLING

ROUND   IN FRONT AND BACK

LET THE SHOULDER GIRDLE REST
ON A ROUND RIB CAGE

LET THE RIBS BE MALLEABLE
TO THE FILLING AND EMPTYING OF THE LUNGS

SEE THE 'RING' OF THE SHOULDER GIRDLE

FILLING WITH THE BREATH

LET THE ARM-PITS BE DEEP / SOFT

LET THE SHOULDERS OPEN

TO ALLOW THE SPINE TO MOVE

UP

THE SCAPULAE ARE A PAIR OF RAFTS
FLOATING ON THE BACK

A MOVING SUPPORT FOR THE MUSCLES
ANCHORING THE ARMS INTO THE WHOLE SPINE

THE ARM HANGS FROM THE SCAPULA

IMAGINE THE SCAPULAE AS EARS
OPENING

L I S T E N I N G

OUT TO THE TIPS OF THE SHOULDERS
IN TO THE CORE OF THE SPINE
DOWN TO THE ARROW OF THE SACRUM

A CLUSTER OF 8 PEBBLE-LIKE BONES
FORM THE BASE OF THE HAND

FROM WHICH 19 LONG BONES OF THE FINGERS EXTEND

HOLD THE BONES OF THE HAND LIGHTLY

LISTEN TO THE VOICES OF ELBOW, SHOULDERS, WRIST

OPEN THE EYE OF EACH FINGER

LONG ARMS   FOLDING / UNFOLDING

BEHIND   ABOVE   AROUND

OPENING INTO THE SPACE AROUND YOU

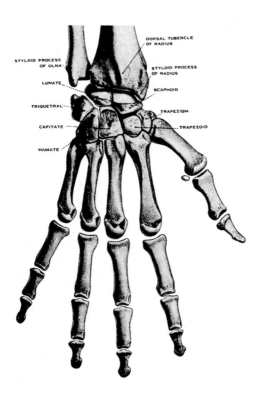

THE LEGS ARE LONG

SEE THE LEGS RELEASING DOWN
FROM THE UNDERSIDE OF THE DIAPHRAGM

PLACE A CUSHION OF AIR

AT HIPS   KNEES   ANKLES

LET THE LIGHT SHINE THROUGH

S O F T E N I N G   3 FOLDS

FROM THE FRONT OF THE HIPS
THROUGH TO THE SIT-BONES

FROM THE BACK OF THE KNEE
THROUGH TO THE FRONT

FROM THE FRONT OF THE ANKLE
THROUGH TO THE HEEL

LET THE KNEE-CAP FLOAT
AN ISLAND ON THE FRONT OF THE KNEE

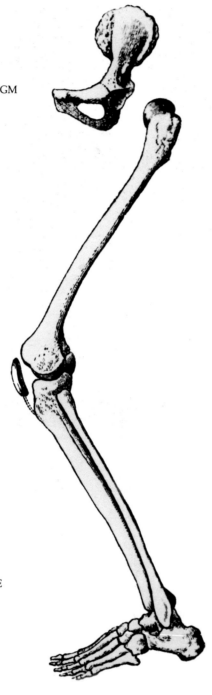

Steve Paxton, *Site*, 1979
Photo Graham Greene

There are two girdles in the body, shoulder and pelvic, through which the limbs connect to the torso. The shoulder sockets are shallow and lie at the outer edge of the body. This allows an extraordinary range of movement. The hip sockets are deep and lie closer to the centre of the body (a hand's breadth apart). They allow only restricted movement because of the supporting function of the legs.

The head directs
the torso is the power house
the arms act upon the world
the legs move the body around.

The weight of the body passes down the spine, spreads out through the pelvis, down the legs and through the feet into the floor. The entire weight of the body meets the floor through the highly articulated and delicate structure of the foot (imagine walking on clubbed feet). Support from the floor rises through the foot and leg right up to the head.

The psoas muscle connects the inner thigh up into the spine as high as the floating ribs and the lower borders of the diaphragm. The legs 'begin' high in the centre of the body.

62 bones make up the lower limbs, the long bone of the femur lengthening into the two bones of the lower leg, tibia and fibula, which open into the 27 bones of each foot. The foot acts as a flexible support and as a lever to propel the body forward.

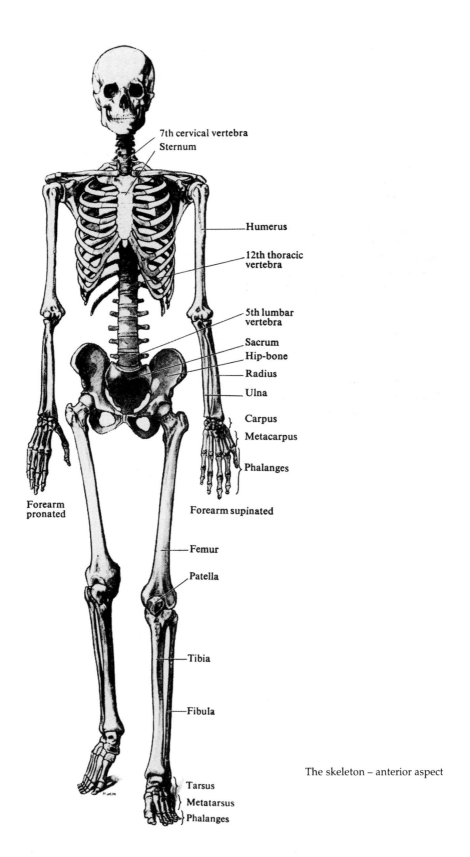

7th cervical vertebra

Sternum

Humerus

12th thoracic vertebra

5th lumbar vertebra

Sacrum

Hip-bone

Radius

Ulna

Carpus

Metacarpus

Phalanges

Forearm pronated

Forearm supinated

Femur

Patella

Tibia

Fibula

Tarsus

Metatarsus

Phalanges

The skeleton – anterior aspect

LET THE FEET BE SOFT

SEE THROUGH THE FLOOR
AS IF IT WERE WATER

IMAGINE THE FLOOR OPENING UP
TO YOUR FEET AS YOU STEP

WALKING BACKWARDS

LET THE HEELS DROP

SOFTEN DOWN THE SPINES OF THE VERTEBRAE

D O W N   THE BACKS OF THE LEGS

TO THE HEELS

LET THE WHOLE HEAD BE FULL

AND MOVING

UP

LEGS SWINGING   FOLDING EASILY

CRAWLING   ROLLING   WALKING   FALLING

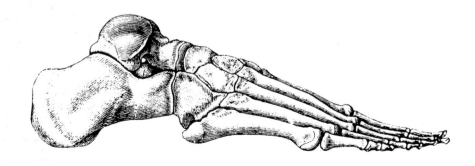

THE BRAIN IS AN ANCIENT LAND FLOATING
BEHIND THE EYES

MOUNTAINS   VALLEYS   CORRIDORS

> In man the brain is more convoluted
> than any other creature, to accommodate
> the billions of cells that make up
> the cerebral cortex.

THE BRAIN ELONGATES INTO THE SPINAL CORD
BRANCHES THROUGHOUT THE BODY

A NETWORK OF SENSES
FANNING OUT FROM THE HEAD
RETURNING TO THE HEAD

> The brain is not a solid mass of tissue
> but a maze of fluid filled corridors.
> The Greeks believed the soul
> was born in the fluids of the brain.

LET THE EYES TAKE THEIR ROOTING FROM THE FEET
LET THE TOES SMELL THE EARTH
LET THE PORES OF THE SKIN BE RESPONSIVE TO THE LIGHT

SIGHT   TASTE   TOUCH   SOUND

REFLECTING THROUGH THE BODY

LETTING THE BODY OPEN IN THE BRANCHING OF THE SENSES

NOTICING THE BOUNDARIES

NOT HOLDING THE CORE
OF OURSELVES TOO TIGHTLY

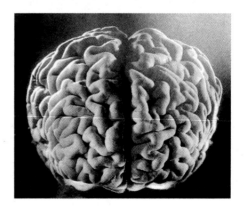

Photos from Lennart Nilsson, *Behold Man*

Branching of nerve cells

2   IMPROVISATION

Max Ernst, plate from *Une Semaine de Bonté*, 1933
© DACS 1989

USES OF IMPROVISATION

1   as a source for original material

2   as training in perception

3   to develop a piece

4   as a performance mode in itself

We improvise the moment we cease to know what is going to happen.

Setting the mind loose from the ongoingness
of everyday life

to find what lies at the edge,
behind our thinking, seeing.

I get up to close the door

I get up . . . where
            who
            why   . . . am I?

Letting the mind float   to find another order
another story

    Alone enter a room
    Place yourself here
    Or there
    Along a line
    Upside down
    Breath loud as a storm
    Stories rise
    And dissolve
    Man with a spoon in his ear

Improvisation provides us with a means to excavating layers of experience,
sensation, character, feeling that we normally rush through or suppress – to
travel deeper and deeper into an ever enlarging and changing moment.

What do we know   that we do not know   we know?

The mind / body   dreams and wanders

As a strategy for discovering and developing images it both demands and
creates a whole range of skills, the most important of which is an ability to be
still and open one's attention to the present moment.

Giorgio de Chirico *Melancholy and Mystery of a Street*, 1914
© DACS 1989

Listening

To myself, and

To my surroundings,
To the song that rises from this moment
in which I am contained –

These dances rise up inside of me
and spin out beneath me,
And it's as if I stand back, inside myself
and observe . . .

Available to constant flow and change,
I can balance
at the edge of the unknown,
and experience fearlessness.

Eva Karczag

Eva Karczag, 1988
Photo Richard Kerry

Photo Hugh Brody

Lie resting

Let the floor be like warm sand

soft   opening   to your body

See the imprint of your body
in the sand

slowly rolling
over different surfaces

leaving a map of the landscape of your body

the most unfamiliar   the unreachable

Let the floor listen
to the messages the body leaves of itself

The air listens to the body

inside   and   outside

Enter the space each day not knowing
what you will find there

Do whatever you need to get comfortable

RUN   YAWN   ROLL

Wake up / energise the different parts

face   fingers   spine   head   toes   ears   ankles   ribs

Warm up exploring the space immediately around the body

under   behind   beyond
at the edge   at the centre

under the feet   above the head   behind the ears
in a bundle   spiralling   moving out and back in

Find new spaces and move into them

Cover a lot of space
each part of the body able to move independently
in any direction

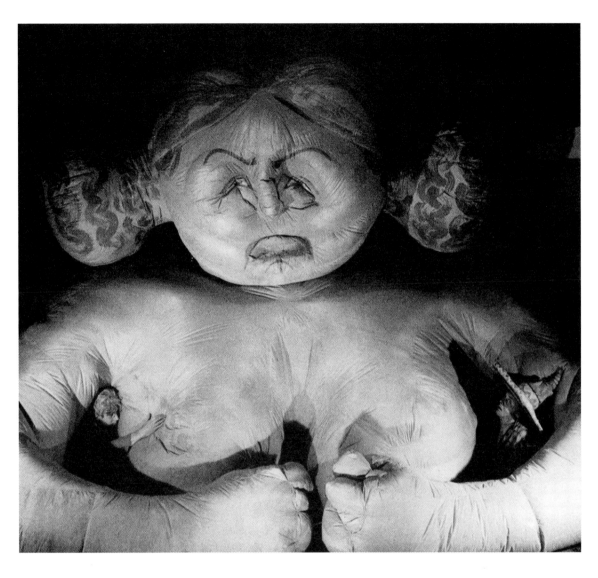

Forkbeard Fantasy, *Myth*, 1986

Miranda Tufnell and Dennis Greenwood with Tim Head, *Vanishing Point*, 1980
Photo Chris Davies

Walking

forwards   backwards   around

slowly

with interruptions

backwards in half circles

sideways

to and fro

Get lost in the walking

here   there   to the edges   in lines / curves

stepping high, low, heavy

exaggerating rhythms

come across a stillness

Listen to the rhythms, sounds, momentum of the stepping

Allow patterns to develop

Pablo Picasso, *Women Running on the Beach*, 1922
© DACS 1989

Race/run fast into the room

sudden changes of direction

surprise yourself with when you change

let go of head   arms
whole body part of the action

Running with the sensation of the horizon
in your body

everywhere in the room

between two points

in your own time coming to rest

How much have you released / is still contained?

Return to running

allow extremes of energy

Miranda Tufnell in *Other Rooms*, 1980
Photo Dee Conway

MAKE A SLOW JOURNEY

between a chair and the floor

from up to down
and returning

Pass through a hundred moments

At any point   a stillness

What is the smallest change to make
a familiar position unfamiliar?

From a stillness

SUDDENLY
without plans

MOVE INTO THE OPPOSITE

        any kind of opposite:

        opposite posture
        opposite type of activity
        opposite image/scale/energy.

no time to think – let the body follow its own thought

SLOWLY FIND YOUR WAY BACK

Lying

Imagine the body covers a whole continent

a whole day to roll from front to back

Photo John and Eliza Forder

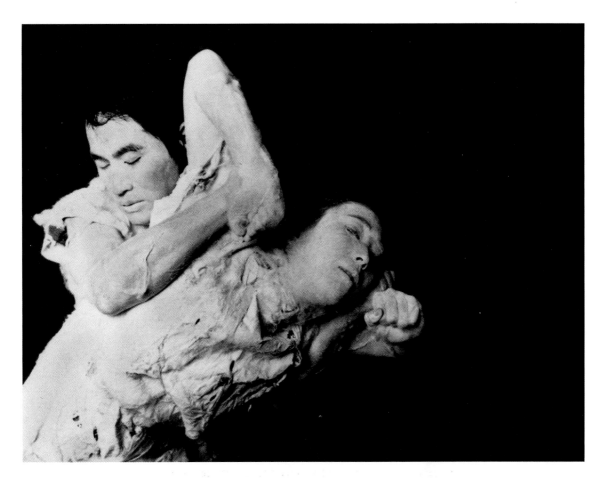

Eiko and Koma in *Trilogy*, 1980/81
Photo Marcus Leatherdale

CONVERSATIONS

In the body

    Begin listening   eyes closed
    listen to the movement of the body/air
    a still dance

    Let one part of the body come to your attention
    a hand
    a foot
    Let its 'voice' emerge in movement
    allow the rest of the body to float/follow

    Listen to the voices of the fingers/toes
    where they want to go
    Offer support from the rest of the body
    hand   wrist   elbow   shoulder   whole body

    Allow these other parts some voice too
    accepting 'disagreements' if necessary

    Enjoy a dialogue between parts of the body
    and its surroundings

In pairs

    A second person adds another 'voice' from outside the body

    by adding touch/pressure a pull a push
    here or there at intervals
    to bring attention to another area
    to give a lead to part of the body:
    shoulder   back of head   heel   inside of thigh

    vary the impact – experiment with direction   speed   force
    The mover may follow/answer/resist/ignore
    let the response be spontaneous

    As a development –

    an imaginary partner offering the external impetus

(derived from Eiko and Koma)

Kirsti Simpson
Photo Bill Arnold

'Where you are when you don't know where you are is one of the most
precious spots offered by improvisation. It is a place from which more
directions are possible than anywhere else. I call this place the Gap. The more I
improvise, the more I'm convinced that it is through the medium of these gaps
– this momentary suspension of reference point – that comes the unexpected
and much sought after 'original' material. It's 'original' because its origin is the
current moment and because it comes from outside our usual frame of
reference.'

Nancy Stark Smith, 'Taking No For An Answer', *Contact Quarterly*, Vol XII No
2, Spring/Summer 87, p3.

CONVERSATIONS
continued

One begins any activity – walking   circling   yawning
Two watches

Two responds (as in a conversation) in any manner while
One watches

Keep alternating   each responding to the other

Allow the possibilities of conversation:
gaps   pauses   both talking at once   monologues   argument

Let the working develop

Try varying whether you respond with
sound   movement   speech   an object:

       I give you a ladder
            you tell me about your favourite landscape
       I command you to be quiet
            you list some popular makes of car
            you turn a somersault
       I construct a wall out of match boxes

Let the other person's movement
trigger an association/fantasy

Find a movement yourself to fit this thought

A travelling conversation between body parts
(your own and others')

         between head and a hand
         knee and an ear
         between right and left side
         between self and object

CALLING AND INTERPRETING INSTRUCTIONS IN PAIRS
(any number of pairs can work simultaneously)

One   gives verbal instructions

The other   interprets/responds in movement

     Sample instructions:

     Sit down
     explore spaces underneath you
     imagine you are moving in thick custard
     do a trick
     run
     be everywhere at once
     be heavy
     roll
     re-arrange the space
     be paper thin
     work in a circle
     inhabit a corner
     find your way back to where you began
     show you are awake

(Objects and furniture may be needed)

As a development   let the instructions loose

     in a group   all/any   calling instructions
                  all/any   responding

CALLING

Watch your partner; build up an interaction. Allow what your partner is doing to influence the type and timing of instructions.

Allow room for interpretation in the instructions, but include variety (some specific, some general, some literal, some qualitative).

Give time for your partner to absorb and explore instructions; experiment with variable timing. Include surprises, for your partner/for yourself.

Explore ways of calling – gentle/abrupt, loud/soft, whispered/roared.

INTERPRETING

Use the instructions as material to feed your own developing action (no need to be a slave).

Give time, allow a pause (however short) before responding.

Try not to know how you will respond (let your body respond without deliberation).

Explore different dimensions of response:

respond quickly and simply, respond elaborately and at length, respond minimally, respond energetically, respond by free association, respond in an opposite sense, choose not to respond at all . . .

If you feel instructions are not working for you (making you feel controlled, leaving things too open, too fast or slow), stop and discuss . . . perhaps swap over for a while.

Avoid miming.

'She runs a race, rides a bicycle, quivers like the early movies, imitates Charlie Chaplin, chases a thief with a revolver, boxes, dances a ragtime, goes to sleep, gets shipwrecked, rolls on the grass on an April morning, takes a snapshot . . .'

Cocteau's instructions for the American Girl in *Parade* – opened 17 May 1917.

Miranda Tufnell and Dennis Greenwood, *Split*, 1984
Photo Chris Ha

EXERCISES FROM CONTACT

In pairs   one goes on all fours
             two hangs over one

Let go of all weight
head   shoulders   knees

Breath lengthening the axes of arms   torso   legs
slowly   melt down off your partner   into the floor

Find a series of stretches supported by your partner
let the hands   feet   head   be like antennae

Find a series of rests supported by your partner
a still or a moving support

A seamless dialogue
exchanging roles   supporting   supported   balancing

Andrew Harwood and Nancy Stark Smith
Photo Bill Arnold

Miranda Tufnell, *Fallout*, 1979
Dancers: Sue Maclennan and Laurie Booth
Photo Dee Conway

Sit back to back with a partner
an 'ear' to the wall of your partner's body
Listen to the ebb and flow
of breath   of weight   of movement

Imagine a bear rubbing its back against a tree
use your partner's back to make your own back:

long   warm   comfortable   wide   flexible

and vice versa

The body is rounded
two round surfaces   meeting   rolling
allow the point of contact to roll
around   down the arms   across the pelvis

Block/resist your partner's movement

Support your partner's movement for five minutes

Slowly fall
into the ground and roll back up into standing

the floor opening as you go down into it

Find a partner
slowly giving way together
falling into the floor
rolling apart and returning to standing

F a l l i n g
at any point   on the way up   or down
alone or with partner(s)

Take a walk   not allowing your partner to fall

Carry/support your partner
all the way to the floor

Fast falls and recovery
falling head   arm   whole body
find the rebound at the bottom of the fall

falling up   flying
from one support to another

IMAGINE YOUR BODY AS   BIG AND FULL OF AIR
AS YOU FALL   AS YOU SUPPORT

GROUPS AND SPACES

The transition from working singly or in pairs to working in a group involves a sharp increase in order of complexity. Group improvisation demands an opening of the attention, both to the work space and to the corpus of people in the space, as an ever-changing pattern of sound, activity, colour and energy. We assume a group which operates in an equal way with no fixed leaders or followers; there are no main or subsidiary parts. There may well be one member of the group who devises the boundaries of action, but once these are set, all participants work equally to realise the possibilities of those boundaries. Similarly it is important that one-to-one relationships within the group are not concerned with power or conformity. Each person is at once responsive to others and independent of them, ready to be changed by, but not absorbed into, another person's activity. The skill lies in being able to include what another person is doing while not losing one's own momentum of thought. This is a fine line and a difficult balance to strike. It is all too easy to make interventions which cut off another person's ability to respond in their own way, or to give up one's own line of thought in preference to another's.

Each person must become an ingredient in the mixing and making of a piece. There is no place for manners or mannerisms. Social conventions, routine habits of polite or impolite daily life, suppress the sensory and imaginative world from which this work begins. Normal social selves must be shed and attention re-directed to the work as a whole. Individuals become a group; the improvisation is a single total event, or succession of events in which each person becomes simply a part. Improvisational groups in which all participants have creative room for manoeuvre are highly productive. But in the onrush of new thought, ideas are often interrupted before they have developed. A key problem is how to stay with an idea or emerging image. This underlines the need to keep watching, to select material and gradually to identify a specific landscape of ideas.

'We were not interested in having ideas about how movements should relate but in looking at how things did relate.'

Simone Forti, *Handbook in Motion*, p32
© Simone Forti, 1974

WALKING

Take a walk   anywhere in the room

note the light   shadow   smell   temperature
How many people   bits of furniture   colours of clothes?

Listen to the sounds of the room   of your breath
the energy of the group

      Where have you come from?
      Are you expecting anything?
      What season is it?
      Where is North?
      What have you missed?
      What boundaries are you setting?

Find a place to stand still

what is in front/at the edge of your vision?

let impressions come   without searching

the   eye   as   a   window

Walking

find places to stand/rest
in the middle   close to the floor   against a wall

any posture   with another person.

Listen to the pattern of:

walking   stillness   grouping   emptiness

André Kertész, New York, September 25, 1969
© Ministère de la Culture et de la Communication, Paris

Walk with a decided destination
surprise yourself with sudden changes of direction

add stillness to your working

Open your attention to the pattern of the group
collisions as interruptions or additions?

Increase the energy of walking   20% 120%
Build to running

Walking on curves/circles – a pattern of circles.

Move into the spaces between people
between people/walls

fill up the empty spaces

move into the spaces around another person
under   beside   behind

running   jumping in

WHEN THE LIMITS HAVE BEEN EXPLORED
ALLOW THE RULES TO CHANGE

Sue MacLennan, *New Moves*, 1983
Photo Emily Barney

Stanley Spencer, *Hilda Welcomed*, 1939/43
Art Gallery of South Australia, Adelaide
Morgan Thomas Bequest Fund 1956

'OVER, UNDER and AROUND'

Over   under   and around
in any order
with any person
or piece of furniture

(a more elaborate version of this, using radios to give cues, may be found in
Simone Forti's *Handbook in Motion* . . . 'When you go to pass under someone he
may also be trying to pass under you or over you . . .')

BODY SCULPTING

One stands

Two moulds self to One's body
(body soft as wax to take an impress)

One leaves
Two remains with residual shape (an empty mould)

One moulds again
etc. . . .

In pairs/groups   capitalise on any developments
listening to the different qualities of each process

stillness   moulding   moving between

FOLLOW MY LEADER
(as a large group)

Begin with walking
at any point   choose your own leader

follow any aspect of their activity
a whole or a part
anticipate your leader

Who is the leader? . . . 7 leaders . . . 1 leader

Someone else may be following *you*

TAKE A BLINDFOLD PARTNER ON A JOURNEY THROUGH THE ROOM

in silence

explore   touch   sound   distance

whatever comes to your attention

>   glass slippery like velvet
>   sound of running water
>   suddenly close to a wall
>   a small hole
>   glare of sun seen through eyelids

Let the sensations   stories   images   rise

and dissolve

Record impressions

and exchange roles

Strategies for using this material:

Inhabit your record of impressions. Use it as a score and source for movement.

Design the objects in the space to echo your score. Inhabit your own arrangement. How/who are you in this place?

Simone Forti with Sally Banes, *Planet*, 1976
Photo Peter Moore

'Mud with fresh moose print, deep and clear the rounded cloven depth signals
great weight. I love to run my fingers in, slip two, one each into two sharp
tips, then draw ten fingers back over the ridge dividing the two parts of the
great hoof.'
Simone Forti

WORKING WITH SPACE

Like silence and stillness we experience space as an absence, an interval or relationship between things.

As we cross a town square, or stand in a crowded bus, we both change and are changed by the space around us. How we walk, sit or stand is influenced by the spaces in which we move. Space includes us; it is seldom the focus of our attention – we don't so much look at it, as look from within it. The sense of space is only partially visual – we experience it also through movement, touch and sound. But in so far as we see space, we see it articulated in light, shade and shadow. Composition of space is intimately connected with concerns of light and lighting.

We respond to proximity and distance and to feelings of openness and enclosure; they recall our earliest experiences in the world. My distance from or closeness to you can be both metaphor and physical fact. Our sense of position and orientation in space – on top, below, behind, left, right – is a way of describing social or psychological relationships as well as spacial ones.

Rosemary Butcher, improvisational studies for *White Field*, 1977
Dancer Dennis Greenwood
Photo Geoff White

Rosemary Butcher, *Flying Lines*, 1987/88

A study of kite flying including sustained periods of running backwards in circles, with many dancers on interlocking and shifting trajectories. Sources for the work included old kite flying manuals with their terminology – looping, tugging, veer to left/right, drifting, etc.

IN ANY NUMBERS

One enters and finds a place/position
Two follows choosing a place in relation to One
and to the space itself
Three follows . . . etc

At any point   change your position   leave   re-enter

What is revealed about the space?
Where is it empty/full . . .?

IN GROUPS

Devise an activity
to make some aspect of the room more visible

50 people jumping in a high room

FILL THE SPACE WITH ACTIVITY

run out of
into
sit in a corner
fly from the ceiling
at the bottom of the room
through the floor

Hijikata, Nikutai ne Hanran (Rebellion of the flesh)

'The performance began with a flying model aircraft which crashed into a huge
metal sheet at the back of the stage after circling over the audience, screeching
with noise. Hijikata appeared, making slow progress through the audience
from the back of the hall, as if he were to be crowned. He was muttering,
groaning, singing – in some way dancing. In a later scene he was suspended
from the ceiling like a moth, as if trapped in a spider's web. This was not
elegant or aesthetic, but wild, vivid, delicate . . . we could say he gave us
"super position" and "super elegant".'

Kō Murobushi, quoted in: Lizzy Slater, *Investigations into Ankoku Butoh*, 1985

ENTERING

Enter

Be prepared to wait
            be lost
            to leave
            to start something new

open to anything – sensations/associations

One thing catches on

on your own   in dialogue   the whole group

amplify   extend   take in other cues   jump into something new

Experiment with different ways of joining another person in a space

Commit yourself to your action at the same time as not
predicting the outcome –

            enter the middle
            enter from an edge   from the back
            enter slowly   or with a run

            go and sit in a corner
            sit with your back to another person
            enter in an assisting role

Enter   not as yourself   but as a fresh ingredient called into being
by the state of affairs in the space at that moment finding a gap that
calls out to be filled*

*This thought contrasts with the theatrical tradition of making an entrance,
where all eyes are upon the drama of the individual actor/character who in
entering takes over the action. Both have possibilities.

'Holding the moment open a few seconds longer widens the gap where the old behaviour/idea/movement/thought/feeling would have gone. And maybe you have nothing to put in its stead. So you put in nothing.'

Nancy Stark Smith, 'Taking No for An Answer', *Contact Quarterly*, Vol XII No 2, Spring/Summer 1987, p3.

Mary Fulkerson, *Dream*, 1982

PARTICULAR DECISION POINTS OCCUR WHEN:

You commit yourself to an action:
on your own   with another person   with an object . . .

At any point:

stay   and find a way through or

leave   to watch or find another situation

You start to feel constrained by what is occurring

Identify the boundaries you are working within

What is needed?   a surprise
                    a change of rhythm
                    an extra person
                    a stillness
                    an exaggeration

Let the work stay on an edge of discovery and uncertainty;
this gives it its life.

There's a choice between:

letting something transform/develop in its own time,
and making a change to avoid the rut of the familiar.

Both strategies are necessary at different times.

STRATEGIES FOR JOINING ANOTHER PERSON'S ACTIVITY

Do the same thing ....

Set up a related activity in harmony with the first ....

Set up a similar activity in rhythmic counterpoint ....

Set up a contrasting activity (that makes the first more visible) ....

Help what is going on (in whatever way you care to interpret the word 'help') ....

Obstruct a person's activity with a contrary one ....

Change the environment within which someone is working ....

Exist in another time or dimension ....

Start simply   run   walk   roll
allow changes in response to what is occurring
(in joining and being joined)

Grade your input – large or small

Conflict as well as collaboration often
gives sharpness to the work

......................................one person walking up and down
                                 two people walking up and down

......................................run up and down and across their path

......................................walk, turn, re-turn in counterpoint

......................................stand still

......................................tow them along with a rope

......................................fill their pathway with furniture
                                 take the object they were working with

......................................switch off the light, turn on the radio

......................................be present as a ghost

WORD PHRASES – MOVEMENT PHRASES

Five minutes continuous whispering and moving
single words   phrases   a continuous monologue
(sense or nonsense)

from this
select phrases of movement/speech that worked together

develop   eg   as a pattern of repeated phrases
                    as conversation
                    as story

Tell yourself the story of your day
move into it

Make a list of phrases noted
on a journey   in a day   while shopping

combine as source for movement

'I changed my mind'
'Why not look over there'
'A lot can happen between now and then'

listen to the sound and rhythm of the words
explore while speaking/moving

vary speed   scale   volume   of words and actions

Tape a statement or a story
use movement to respond to the rhythm of the words

Katy Duck, 'Group O', *Mind the Gap*, 1986
Photo Anneliese Wolf

KATY DUCK, ON THE BREADLINE, 1984
Get Up and Go Rap (to be improvised with)

'Get up, go go go wait, OK wait, come on I'll do it, right, what happened now?
What a mess! Let me do it, OK, then you go, wait, no I have to get it. You can
ask her? OK, is it ready? Put it in the car, let's go, wait, there we go, finally.
Where are they? I don't know. OK then just sit the thing down, they'll come
mmmmmmm, what time is it? I don't know. Want a cigarette? Yea – it's cold
too. Here I brought some sandwiches, is that them? No, OK I'll have one now
and the other later. Give me a light. Lots of wind today. Yes, where are they? I
don't know. Give me another piece. It's finished. We can go to the store before
they get here. But they're already late. I know but we're here! OK you go, I'll
wait. God could I use a coke. I'll get some. Bring me a sweater too. Wait, last
one in the pack, shit! I should've told her. Oh there they are. Where have you
been? Just a traffic jam, your sister? She's coming. Got a cigarette? Yea here.
Hope she hurries up. There she is – with a basket. Hi, we were waiting. You
want a coke? No, we gotta get going.'   Katy Duck

From working papers for *On the Breadline*, 1984, based on the tragedy of Lenny
Bruce. Work devised for Extemporary Dance Theatre.

VOICE

Forms of speech if freed from the necessity for literal meaning, can be explored in their own right for what they may evoke. Since much of one's own identity is carried in voice, accent, turn of phrase, some work may be needed to explore beyond these personal signatures.

Reading from any text
Consider possibilities of:

SOUND, SPACE, RHYTHM

Speak very loud/declamatory   soft/confidential

with female/male voice   varying extremely high/low

with an aid: cardboard cone   gag   microphone . . .

Speak from far away/from nearby

listen to your own voice
in a confined space   out of doors   in a cathedral

Listen to the sounds/rhythms of the words and phrases
allowing meanings buried in the words to surface

Explore changes of emphasis   dynamic
repetition

Record as score for use in movement

CONVERSATION/FANTASY

In a group

all independently imagine a place/a circumstance

up a tree   under a floor board

One speaks conversationally from within their imagined setting

     'this wind is cooling the pudding'

Another replies from their own setting
letting the first remark influence what they are imagining

     'Why didn't you nail down the floor properly?'

Gradually a shared place or circumstance is nursed
into existence from an extended conversation

(derived from Katy Duck)

THE VOICE OF MEMORY

'The experience of words entering spaces, nervous system reading, knowing throughout minute hairs and threads within my body – the sense of the language, knowing the beginning and the end of knowing – the angel of information hanging in the air above my soul moving within sentences.'

'I struggle with sentences of insight and try to place myself within the words, within the actions of the words within the references of the words, within the sensations of the words, within the ultimate knowing of the spirit soul of communication and it is so simple. So economical. When I write, do I not fall into the abyss of language and forget where once I knew just my body.'

Mary Fulkerson. Excerpts from *The Book of Fancy Images*, Vol 2, 1989.

PLATO'S CHAIR
excerpt

'Suddenly I felt an enormous tiredness coming over me, I felt a great wave of slumber and sleep sweep through me and I flung my immensely large body on my even bigger bed and I dreamt a dream of such magnitude that it thrust me through into a completely different career. In my dream I was walking along a very very long road. On either side of the road there were trees, it was a sort of copse, a little glade. The leaves on the trees they fluttered as I passed as if a breeze had blown through the trees. On every branch of every tree there was a bird, its wings folded, its beak tucked into its breast and they had all fallen into a deep slumber. The birds all seemed to be sleeping the sleep of the very universe and I knew, I just knew that I mustn't stop and watch this sight, that I must just keep walking along this road. As I walked night fell and I kept walking along the road until I came to a large clearing. I was on the edge of a glade and at the beginning of a clearing and in the middle of the clearing there was a high fence. The fence was made of wire and it was very high and I knew, I knew, I was almost driven, it was as if something was driving me through the fence and I leapt over the fence, I leapt up, I was like a bird, I was like a gazelle, I leapt over the fence and I landed lightly and fleet of foot at the base of the fence. Ahead of me I could see a small wooden hut. It was a military sort of hut. It was like a Nissen hut and on the door of the hut there was the word 'Museum' and I knew categorically that I must be nearing a museum. Quickly I opened the door of the museum and I stepped inside and at this stage, as I was nearing the inside of the building I realised that this was a furniture museum. It was full of items of furniture – chairs, tables, cupboards, wardrobes – that sort of thing. They were all covered by a layer of dust and cobwebs. They had been in there for years. But I knew that in this museum there was an object waiting just for me. So I walked down the museum, I didn't look at the catalogues, I didn't browse through the postcards first, no, I just kept walking to the very end of the museum and there I came across a chair. When I saw this chair I knew that it was for me. On this chair were the words 'Plato's Chair' and so I stole it. I stole the chair and I took it home. I took this chair home and I placed it in my room and I sat in it and I knew that the chair and the dream were some sort of celestial sign, it was some sort of indication that I had to give up my career as a comedian, frankly floundering, and become a philosopher. That wasn't quite what I had in mind for my life, but because I'd got a few gigs lined up I thought I'd sort of weld the two together and that is what I've been trying to do tonight.'

Rose English

Rose English, *Plato's Chair*, 1983/4
Photo Genevieve Cadieux

NARRATIVE

Telling stories to ourselves and to each other about what is happening is part of our relation to the world; a primary dimension of everyone's daily activity which confirms or even creates reality for ourselves and others.

Narrative shapes experience in time; it ties beginnings to endings. Experience itself is seldom a featureless chain of events; birth and death, breathing in and out, confer shape on our existence and already suggest the seeds of narrative form.

Narratives may provide sources for the work; they may arise from within it; or they may shape it over all.

When narratives come from within the work they add another dimension to what is occurring – associations, memories, histories, build upon and extend what is immediately present.

The last hundred years of experiment with narrative and non-narrative forms, the existence of film and TV in modern history, and the influence of poetic and image-based modes of thought on performance, have opened the way to extreme freedom in the treatment of narrative. The logical and linear structure of narrative can exist as mere suggestion in forms akin to dream in which drastic shifts of time, scale, context, style of narrative, can be accommodated, linked as often by poetic association as by literal course of events. Narrative can be subjected to all kinds of fragmentation and distortion, where the whole may be condensed into a single moment or series of moments, stretched out to immense scale or broken up and reassembled like a collage.

TEXT AS QUARRY

A source for material is found from a given text:

      biography
      newspaper article
      magazine story
      oral history

See the text as a quarry from which to draw images

immersing oneself in the material
lifting elements/qualities of interest

letting a sequence of images grow, dissolve, re-combine

(not just illustrating the material . . . absorbing it, taking it further)

ORANGE MAN
A performance by Group/O

The primary study was of the film *The Tin Drum* which was used for its gestures and activities, as a basis for the choreography. The cast was given a story, The Orange Man, written by the director, who had split the story into parts that allowed the cast to work in different groupings on small sections. Each section was improvised by way of the story line, relating the movement to that of the film. By the end of two weeks there was a rough arrangement for a choreography which followed the line of the story and suggested the film by way of movement qualities.

Katy Duck

Jacky Lansley, *The Breath of Kings*, 1986
Photo Jessica Loeb

THE BREATH OF KINGS

'I had been listening to a tape of Richard II, at this time, which was during the America–Libya crisis. I thought the language of Richard II was extremely beautiful, and it had the kind of richness that I always look for in movement. Also the rhythms of it interested me. So I decided to take this very revered bit of theatrical culture, and bring it to life through dance and movement. The piece isn't a remake of Richard II, I'm using the material from the play to talk about other issues – such as the role of women in traditional theatre.'*

The rich emotional power of the words combined with an integrated and refined physical language are used to describe not only the humiliation of a usurped king but also the absence of a female relationship to power.

Giving the words of Shakespeare to women obviously changes the emphasis and meaning, revealing a subtext which is not necessarily in discord with the intention of the play, as Richard is described as a very 'feminine' man who ultimately lays down his arms and gives up the fight. He is 'soft' and resorts in his youth to stereotype female tactics of manipulation, plotting and conspiracy; tactics which women are often forced into as their only form of power. The actresses in my piece 'The Breath of Kings' use these conspiratorial tactics to change events and subvert the meaning of the words.

The juxtaposition of the two Dukes, Bolingbroke and Northumberland with Qadafi and Reagan highlighted the continuous historical obsession with war, placing the female king in the role of a constructive arbitrator and conveyer of peace.

My work aims to create a sense of total theatre within a movement based situation. For the performers, this requires an understanding of the psychological motivation behind movement and taking this into a performance and devising context.

The work is concerned with the whole self in performance so that any gesture, whether naturalistic or stylised, carries within it a sense of historical information and life experience.

Essentially, physical language frees the imagination in relation to known things.

I am interested in exploring the profound issues which affect our lives. The task seems to be to evolve an imaginative theatrical language which can provide a contradiction to the distressing or difficult aspect of a theme. A kind of balance which allows an audience to engage more directly and emotionally with the issue that the work is exploring.

Jacky Lansley

*From an interview with Andy Solway in New Dance, No 39, 1987

AUTOBIOGRAPHY

I was born ....

My first memories are ....

I remember my mother ....

In my dreams I used to ....

I love ....

I have been to ....

Since five o'clock this morning I have ....

What interests me now is ....

I cannot understand why ....

I wish ....

(inspired by Remy Charlip)

Lists of objects/activities/qualities from your past
speak associations from this onto tape
use selected parts as performance score

A public and a private event for each year of your life

List all the roles you play or have played

Walk the journey of your life through the space

A journey through your own body as a landscape

Take a piece of charcoal/pen/pastel
Attending to the sensation in your hand
draw an impression of the inside of your body
how it feels

Use the sketch as a 'score' and find movement to
explore the image drawn

Eleanor Antin as Eleanora Antinova (left) with Anna Cancpa at the Russian Tea Room,
New York City, 1980
Photo Mary Swift

One of her 'life' performances in which she became Eleanora Antinova the black ballerina
for three weeks, keeping a journal throughout. 'I never appeared in public except as a
black ballerina.' The journal was subsequently published.
Eleanor Antin, *Being Antinova*, Astro Artz, 1983

The life performances when I lived as Antinova for three weeks in NY back in
1980 was not like most of my work – with the exception of my king piece when
(weekly for two years) I walked around Salona Beach in California as my
bearded king and got to know the people and their problems. Usually my work
is more theatrical. In the two life performances I did, my intention was to
ground my theatrical personas in the real world, since they were actually very
related to my life but so transformed as not to appear autobiographical to
others. It helped me to place my skin out there in the world and not just my
imagination and did, I think, teach me a great deal about myself and others,
especially in the case of Antinova, the black ballerina, about some of the day to
day irritations, insecurities and pleasures of being black.

Eleanor Antin, 1989.

sounds of heart beats of breath of conversation of weather of dreams

of battles of children of trains – *in the space* of a room of a house of a

street of a town of a country of a continent of a planet – *story* of a moment

of a day of a year of a life of a generation of an era – *voices* of friends

of family of news of ghosts of animals – *seeing* with the eyes of parents

of grandparents of ancestors

Kasuo Ohno, *Admiring La Argentina*, 1984
Photo Nourit Masson-Sekine

'When performing this dance Ohno feels that he is La Argentina,
the famous Spanish dancer he first saw in 1929.'

IMAGES OF CHANGE

organic growth   exponential growth   building in increments

evolution   transformation   erosion   merging

drift   tailing off   breaking up   melting

change of mind   change of rules   change of ingredients

MEASURES OF TIME

sleeping/waking   for the length of a breath
to a point of exhaustion   to boil an egg
time standing still   the time it takes to forget

WHEN IS IT TIME TO MOVE INTO SOMETHING ELSE,
TO CHANGE YOUR THOUGHT?

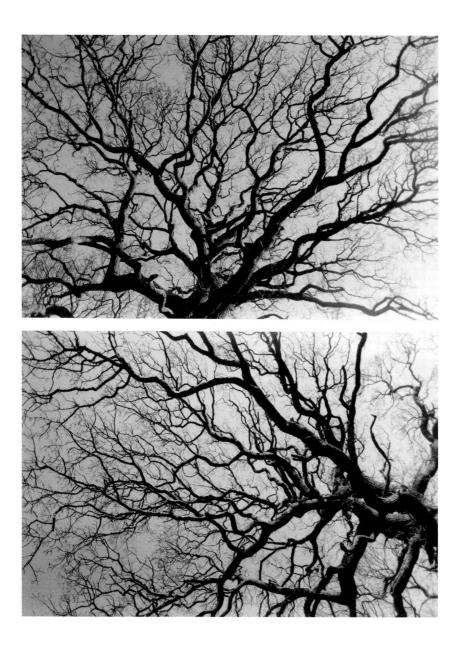

As dancers, we have come forward very strongly in the last twenty or thirty years on a very intuitive and kinesthetic thread. I feel it's imperative now for me to engage in understanding how it is that we relate with our history and how things have happened, how we take our place in a very complex society.

Simone Forti interviewed by Claire Hayes.
'Dancing in Earth Context', *Contact Quarterly*, Vol XII, No 2, Spring/Summer 1987, p10.

FINDING SOURCES IN EXISTING FORMS

Conventions are transformed and enter a new exploratory existence when taken out of their normal context or used in unusual combinations:

Ballroom dancing as performance art (Marty St James and Anne Wilson)

A ballet performed on a stool (Fergus Early)

A dance, film clips, abstract slides, poetry reading, pouring water between two buckets, reading a text on Zen Buddhism, radio sounds, music for prepared piano, playing of exotic musical instruments, gramophone records . . . all mixed together with systematically random timings.
(Untitled event at Black Mountain College 1952, John Cage and others.)

Sometimes the mode of thought that goes with one medium can usefully be transferred to another. This may include applying spacial ideas and perceptions to time structures or conceiving spaces in terms of how they unfold through time.

arranging words as if they were furniture in a space

group improvisation in movement as if it were sculpture

a space composed as if it were music

Gary Stevens, *If the Cap Fits*, 1987
Photo Georgina Carless

If the Cap Fits is in two parts. Each part has a distinctive character. The first part is sculptural, the second makes reference to pantomime. The first part ends with the performers unable to get into another piece of clothing, the second begins as if this process had continued impossibly. I think of myself as a sculptor negotiating the theatre.

My work is informed by the vaudeville tradition and its development into cinema. Many of the jokes and much of the appeal of early silent film comedies was based on the inference of a mind and its nature through the behaviour of the protagonist. The performers/characters were curious thinking objects and their performance drew a distinction between the subject as a conscious agent and a person as an object, be it psychological, historical, social, economic, physical, etc. My work doesn't attempt to imitate those comedies but to reinvent that tradition and its representations.

Gary Stevens

Welfare State Company summer school in processional theatre, 1984.
Students show their work at the local steam rally after a ten day residential course.
Photo Paul Rees

WELFARE STATE

'Its blend of several arts – theatre, performance, ceremony, ritual, sculpture, mime, puppetry, music – makes its productions hard to categorise. There are echoes of Fellini as well as Breughel, Brecht along with Kropotkin, William Morris with Chaucer. Hi-tech blends with medieval folk culture, grand spectacle with participatory processions. If any single thread runs through all its activities, it is a steadfast refusal to provide consumerist theatrical fodder.'

Mike Westlake, *Arts Express*, Oct 1987

IMPROVISATION

SHEDDING

shed self image, plans, worries, socialised behaviour
ask questions – who or what you are/can become
see your relation to the whole
   (yourself as just one ingredient in a whole piece)

BEING RECEPTIVE

be present – keep your attention bright
   (don't lose receptivity when in action)
give time, waiting
   (if necessary past the point of boredom)
let things draw attention to themselves
   (the eye as a window)

ALLOWING

accept stillness/silence/emptiness
   if nothing occurs to you do nothing
accept very small impulses towards action
attend to edges of awareness, the unimportant
capitalise on anything going
a mistake is an opportunity

EXPLORING

accept getting lost
   (journey without a map)
leave something when it becomes too recognisable
take imaginative risks
   (what if . . .?)
take ideas to extremes
the unfamiliar often lies close to the familiar

COMPOSING

be specific and limit your material to get the most out of it
energise the whole space
don't lose your sense of the whole while working on a part
stillness/silence/emptiness balance action

3 LANDSCAPES

If I look at a cup I can name it, I can describe its design. I may be able to guess its value or describe its particular use. This is the everyday shorthand by which I orientate myself and make sense of the world around me.

In another vein of thought I may look at the cup and think of breakfast – a kind of first order association by which I logically connect a cup with a process or event of which a cup is a part.

Lastly I may look and see mainly a white curving shape. It might remind me of a bath or a seagull. I suspend my habits of vision – I let the object settle in my mind as an object and allow images to well up around it.

It is in this last mode of seeing that all this work is located.

'A heavy gypsy with an untamed beard and sparrow hands, who introduced himself as Melquiades, put on a bold public demonstration of what he himself called the eighth wonder of the learned alchemists of Macedonia. He went from house to house dragging two metal ingots and everybody was amazed to see pots, pans, tongs, and braziers tumble down from their places and beams creak from the desperation of nails and screws trying to emerge, and even objects that had been lost for a long time appeared from where they had been searched for most and went dragging along in turbulent confusion behind Melquiades' magical irons. 'Things have a life of their own,' the gypsy proclaimed with a harsh accent. 'It's simply a matter of waking up their souls.'

Gabriel Garcia Marquez, *One Hundred Years of Solitude*, Penguin, 1972

'We see the tea bowl

And don't hear it

A stone is a stone but

A stone can hear you.'

Quoted from *Echo – The Images of Sound*, ed. Panhaysen, 1987, Het-Apollo Huis Eindhoven

CONVERSATIONS WITH AN OBJECT

Choose an object
pass it to and fro between you
listen to it   discover its qualities

Each time
find a different relationship to it
let the object reveal itself

Attend to fleeting thoughts
at the edge of your consciousness

Pass a cup as:
an ear trumpet   a cave   a cold surface . . .

Find a place for an object
a place for yourself in relation to it
listen to it   ignore it   transform   discard

'Read' objects as a score
Imagine them giving you instructions

Find a relationship to an object
find another
find ten more
push yourself beyond 1st   2nd   3rd   thoughts
into unfamiliar territory
100 relationships?

See the object as a person   or an expression

Invent a narrative which includes the object as you work with it

Ordinarily objects are at our disposal
Change roles
perform *for* an object

John Davies, *Old Enemy*, 1973/5
Photo Jorge Lewinsky

A GROUP OF PEOPLE
EACH WITH A FEW SIMPLE OBJECTS
eg 3 sticks

Choose your own space in the room

start from resting

follow any impulse to interact with the objects
let one action flow into the next (be prepared to do nothing)

let the objects be your equal
acting on them and being acted upon by them

Gradually

allow the activity of others
on the periphery of your vision
to influence what you are doing

Develop into
direct interaction with others
the objects becoming 'common property'

At any point
if you lose hold of your own impulse towards action
or if you are unable to take in what is happening
return to stillness or working alone

Tall thin black rods (about chest high) were stood on end in a large space. The performers (about 20 of them) walked to and fro in the space in straight lines. When one performer met a standing pole, the pole fell, making a sharp slapping noise as it hit the floor. All movement froze in that moment until the pole had been balanced on its end again.

Anthony Howell, The Theatre of Mistakes, *Preparation for Displacement*, 1975, described from memory by Chris Crickmay.

'Water was transferred from a bucket on the ground to another at the top of the set of tables and chairs by means of cups. The piece was essentially an additive counting game and cues were given by a chant which the whole group did together. The number of performers was additive too: it increased by one every day over a period of 48 days.'

Anthony Howell, The Theatre of Mistakes, *A Waterfall*, 1977, described by Stuart Morgan in *The Death and Rebirth of British Performance*.

Georg Scholz *Cacti and Semaphore*, 1923
Westfälisches Landesmuseum
für Kunst und Kulturgeschichte, Münster

OBJECTS – A LANDSCAPE

Objects provide a means of building a place within which to improvise – a means to a dialogue with something other than yourself.

You start to compose a landscape within which an event can take place without necessarily knowing what kind of event it will be. But as you begin to assemble objects you are already discovering something about its dimensions and qualities.

Shaping and reshaping the landscape is an integral part of improvisation. People act upon their world and are acted upon by it, a constant dialogue.

ASSEMBLE A KIT

Enter a place full of objects/materials
available for use –

attic   sea shore   derelict building

Spend time there   silently   without searching
without an idea

Let objects draw attention to themselves

Select one thing
add another that feels compatible

continue until you have enough

Make 'heaps' of related things
for one or more pieces of work

Each brings
A 'GIFT' FOR THE GROUP
found or made   single or multiple   permanent or transient

combine or use separately as a kit

Objects from
DIFFERENT CONTEXTS
of use or meaning

fan, oar, riot shield

THE IMPOSSIBLE
a cabbage suit
a thousand owls

Objects that recall
A PAST MOMENT OR EVENT

find objects that fit
the feel of the memory

Select according to
SIMILARITY OR CONTRAST OF

size   shape   texture   colour . . .

Objects/materials that are
EASILY MANIPULATED OR
TRANSFORMED

a large cloth:
hang it up   roll up in it
cover a table   drag it about
wear it . . .

What I do as a 'happening' is part of my general concern, at this time, to use more or less altered 'real' material. This has to do with *objects*, such as typewriters, ping-pong tables, articles of clothing, ice-cream cones, hamburgers, cakes, etc, etc – whatever I happen to come into contact with. The 'happening' is one or another method of using *objects in motion*, and this I take to include people, both in themselves and as agents of object motion.

Claes Oldenburg in Kirby, M, *Happenings*, Dutton, 1965, p200

The lower the 'rank' of an object, the greater its chances for revealing its objective character . . .

This is why among my 'works' I can list such as: a store of rubbish, a cloakroom like shambles, people hanging in a wardrobe, a learned dispute on a heap of coal, a mad girl with teaspoons . . .

Tadeusz Kantor, 1961, in Piotr Graff, trans, *Emballage*, Galeria Foksal PSP Books, 1976.

Mary Fulkerson and Chris Crickmay, *Field*, 1981/2
Photo Graham Greene

We began with two enormous floor coverings, a dozen large poles (as cut from the woods), long lengths of rope, small bags stuffed with sawdust, and an old laundry basket. We built structures and improvised movement in a long succession of rehearsals. Soon we added sound tapes and slide projectors, slides of a field being harvested and then a dance film, made previously, set in various landscapes. Later we cut up some remnants of the film and collaged them together to project as slides. Exotic costumes were added (eg a suit of plastic grass), and finally a reading from Berger's essay *Field*. The projectors were set at floor level within the performance area projecting onto two flanking walls. The large size of the slide images made for continuous changes in the scale and quality of the space. The final piece was improvised throughout within broad sections marked by changes of sound, costume or projected material. It started small and still and became more complex and involved as it went on.

Rose Garrard, *Tumbled Frame*, 1985, Installation

ARRANGE OBJECTS IN A SPACE

DEFINE   WORK SPACE   AND   VIEWING SPACE

Work space starts empty
Viewing space contains a chosen collection of objects

Working as a group   in silence

CREATE A LANDSCAPE OF OBJECTS

ADD   MOVE   REMOVE   elements

taking turns to enter the work space

WATCH THE IMPACT OF EACH CHANGE UPON THE WHOLE

KEEP TRANSFORMING THE ARRANGEMENT

Keep the whole space energised – any dead areas?

Balance occupied space with emptiness.

What is the smallest change that will alter the whole?

Tomb of the First Emperor, Mount Li, China

AS DEVELOPMENTS:

ALLOW STORIES TO ARISE OUT OF THE MATERIAL
and influence the arranging
Accept the fantastic/the improbable
whatever occurs to you
an inner story you tell to yourself

'that chair is smiling'
'messages are travelling down this string'

INCLUDE PEOPLE-AS-OBJECTS IN THE ARRANGEMENT
a static tableau
until they decide to leave the space

arranger places and moulds
person being arranged becomes clay

LET A SINGLE PERSON ARRANGE THE SPACE AT THE START
Others then use it as a landscape for improvisation
changing it as they work

OR group divides into:
ARRANGERS   PERSONS-AS-OBJECTS   PERFORMERS
all proceed simultaneously

Add the ingredients of light and sound *(see later)*

THE MAIN DEVELOPMENT FROM THIS POINT IS TO ADD OTHER ELEMENTS OF
IMPROVISATION SO THAT ARRANGING OBJECTS BECOMES PART OF A LARGER
PROCESS

NOTES ON ARRANGING OBJECTS

In order to get anywhere with this work it is worth bearing the following points in mind:

In selecting objects consider:
Range of *scale* (small to big), avoiding gaps in the range.
A combination of things you *like*.

In defining the work space, make clear the *edges* – some should be walls.

Viewing is as important an activity as arranging.
Work slowly enough for everyone to take in the changes.

Take account of the *given* features of the space as well as what you may add: a crack in the plaster, a mark on the floor, a step, a window.
If things all end up in the middle you have probably lost your sense of the space itself.

Work as *equally* as possible (not one or two people in the group dominating).
Respect other people's efforts, but not so much that you can't change anything.
Work in silence, then stop for discussion.

There is no need to work *naturalistically* to set a scene. The objects in your arrangement are simply sculptural elements. This also applies if you extend the work to include people-as-objects.

Keep the space in a state of *transformation*. If it starts to become too fixed, make small or large changes to move it on.

Allow the work to continue in its *own time*, eventually coming to a natural conclusion,
Or break off – clear the space – and start again.

Repeat the process often enough to go beyond first ideas so that you begin to really *see* your material. Each time start from scratch with an empty space.
The energy coherence and inventiveness of the work will rise dramatically once the group's receptivity and attention has had a chance to build.

Watch for major areas of choice that you may be *neglecting*: doors open or closed? lights? floor surface? orientation of objects (upside down, sideways, leaning)? anything excluded as too boring? too difficult?

TRACES OF PROCESS

In everyday settings, collections of objects often look coherent, not because they have been composed, but because a coherent, living process has occurred amongst them –

> Tracks left by animals in snow
> Craftsman's workshop
> Ants' nest patterns
> Table after a meal

When we arrange things deliberately we commonly resort to simple patterns – a circle, a square, a line, a pile, various forms of symmetry, things at right angles to each other . . . Arrangements that emerge through a living process tend not to lend themselves to such overall descriptions.

AS PART OF AN IMPROVISATION,
ALLOW THE WORK PROCESS TO FORM ITS OWN ARRANGEMENTS
WATCH THE PATTERNS THAT EMERGE IN THE SPACE

Libby Dempster in rehearsal with Little Theatre
(a group collaboration initiated by Mary Fulkerson), 1980
Photo Chris Crickmay

PORTRAIT WITH OBJECTS

Choose a person in the group
(without saying who it is)

Going round the circle
Each in turn names a category
eg colours   sounds   items of clothing   animals

For each category named
write down what your chosen person would be

time of day 6am
plant ....thistle
building ....garden shed

When you have a long enough list
use it as a starting point for choosing:

OBJECTS
A PLACE
AN ARRANGEMENT

Enter this setting to make a short 'performance portrait'
or tableau.

RANDOM NOTES ON RAUSCHENBERG'S
SPRING TRAINING (1965). WITH
TRISHA BROWN, LUCINDA CHILDS,
CHRISTOPHER RAUSCHENBERG,
STEVE PAXTON, AND ROBERT
RAUSCHENBERG, AND A LARGE NUMBER
OF DESERT AFRICAN TORTOISES (WHICH
WILL BE CALLED 'TURTLES' IN THIS TEXT.)
LIGHTING BY JENNIFER TIPTON. MUSIC:
VARIOUS.

THE PREMIER WAS IN A LARGE ABANDOND
TELEVISION STUDIO. IT HAD A GLASSY
CONCRETE FLOOR, AND THE LIGHTING
GRID PUT A DARK METAL CAP ON THE
SPACE ABOUT 25 FEET UP. POSSIBLY
150 PEOPLE WATCHED.

THE LIGHTS CAME UP IN AN EMPTY SPACE.
EXPECTANT EYES SEARCHED LEFT AND RIGHT.
PLOP. ON THE VAST PERFECT FLOOR, A
SMASHED LITTLE ISLAND OF EGG. ANOTHER.
EYES RAISED. A SHADOW MOVED ABOVE
THE GRID.

FURTHER LIGHTS GLOWED, AND THE
BRIDES WANDERED IN THE AISLES
MUNCHING ABSTRACTEDLY ON CRACKERS.
PUSHING A SHOPPING CART FULL OF
TICKING CLOCKS. AN ALARM WENT OFF.
A CLOCK WAS PRODUCED FROM THE BOSOM
OF A WEDDING GOWN, AND THE ALARM
QUIETED.

ON STAGE A MAN'S SOLO BEGAN. I
SUPPOSE I WAS CONVENTIONALLY
DRESSED FOR DANCING EXCEPT FOR
A KNEEPAD ON ONE KNEE, TO WHICH
WAS WIRED A LARGE TIN CAN. UPON
THIS CAN I ROTATED MY WAY OFF-
STAGE IN THE FINAL MOMENTS.

A LARGE WHEELED BOX WITH CANVAS
SIDES WAS PUSHED IN BY CHRISTOPHER.
THE DARKNESS DEEPEND. LIGHT AND SHADOWS
FROM WITHIN THE BOX — OR, POSSIBLY, BLACK
SHAPES WERE WITHDRAWN, PLACED ON THE
FLOOR, AND THE SWITCH THROWN ON FLASHLIGHTS
MOUNTED ON THE MOUNDED BACKS OF THE
TURTLES. THEY BEGAN TO WALK.

TURTLES WALK LIKE JUGGERNAUTS BUT
STRAIN FOREWARD LIKE GREY-
HOUNDS. CAUGHT IN EACH
OTHER'S LIGHT OR IN THEIR
OWN, THEY BEGAN SLOW PROGRESS
TOWARD THE AUDIENCE. SHADOWS
ON THE WALLS REVEALED MAGNI-
FIED REPTILIAN NECKS AND HEADS
AS LARGE AS HIPPOS, BUT CRAGGY
AND PHALLIC.

THE DUET INCLUDED A GAME WITH
TWO MOVEMENT POSSIBILITIES
AND ONE RULE: BOTH MOVEMENTS
MUST BE ALWAYS PRESENT. WHEN
RAUSCHENBERG WAS ON TIPTOE, I
SHOULD BE WALKING OR RUNNING.
THE RULE PROVOKED A RIVALRY FIRST,
THEN A COMPLICITY EVOLVED, FOLLOWED
BY A COMMUNICATION. THE DUET
ENDED WITH A SERIES OF LIFTS IN
WHICH ONE WENT RIGID AND WAS
CARRIED TO ANOTHER SPACE, CROSS-
BODY. WHEN PUT DOWN ON FEET,
THE RIGID MAN PICKED UP THE
CARRIER IN THE CARRY, AND TRANS-
PORTED HIM.

RAUSCHENBERG ENTERED ON
WOODEN STILTS, ILLUMINATED
HERE AND THERE BY TURTLE-LIGHT.
HE WORE A PLAID FLANNEL
SHIRT AND JOCKEY SHORTS. HIS
LONG-BONED FEET PROTRUDED
IN BOTH DIRECTIONS OVER THE
STRUTS OF THE STILTS. THERE
WERE CLUNKY WOODEN STEPS
BETWEEN TURTLES AND EGGS.

AND IN A SPOTLIGHT AT THE
RIGHT OF THE STAGE, RAUSCHENBERG
WAS CLAD IN A WHITE DINNER
JACKET. FROM HIS WAIST DEPENDED
A ROPE, SUSPENDING A BUCKET
BETWEEN HIS LEGS. FROM THE
LIP OF THE BUCKET FUMED
WHITE CO_2 GAS. HAWAIIAN
MUSIC. SMALL MOVEMENTS IN THE
RIGHT WRIST.

STEVE PAXTON
1989

Steve Paxton, memories of Rauschenberg's *Spring Training*, 1965

ROOMS

Mary had the idea that each of us would start by inventing a 'room', which singly or together would become environments for performance. These rooms were put together over several days without any of us knowing what the others were planning. The rooms that emerged had the following ingredients:

Miranda: table, wooden chair, basket chair, desk lamp, together with phrases from a poem she had written entitled, 'a room with a view'.
'growing old in the middle of all that furniture'
'what reason for going – or not going – out?'
This room was conceived as a night-time space 3–5am.

Mary: a small collection of slides of paintings by Paul Wiesefelt. The paintings were of interiors done in a super-realist manner. Mary's room also included conversations with the painter concerning his work. Slides were projected large or small onto the available surfaces in the work space.

Chris: extracts from the story of Rumpelstiltskin taken from an edition illustrated by David Hockney. In the story a girl is set the seemingly impossible task of turning straw into gold. The room included a stack of 12 bales of straw. A typical phrase from the book was the hopeful remark, 'a lot can happen between now and then'. This and other phrases were repeated aloud and became commentaries on the action.
One of our interests was to extend our own sense of possibility. The straw was chosen partly to enlarge the scale and increase the ruggedness of our work. But early experiments with undoing the bales of straw proved chaotic and it was later used simply as a stack.

Dennis: two photographs of an old neglected garden with statues, fountains, etc, suggesting a view from a window.

Libby: several small bags tied together so that they could be worn on the body. The bags contained objects evoking a person's past – small books, photographs, a scarf, some stones. They suggested the 'room' of a traveller. In working on this room, people lay on the floor like stones, loaded bags onto each other, etc. The whole seemed to evoke a death/archaeology/debris left behind.

We took each 'room' and worked on it as a group. The originator set out their material in the work space. Others then inhabited the room and explored its character through improvisation. Later the rooms were combined to make an improvised performance.

(A collaboration between Mary Fulkerson, Miranda Tufnell, Chris Crickmay, Libby Dempster and Dennis Greenwood. This was the second piece produced under the title, 'Little Theatre'. It was performed at the Dartington Dance Festival 1980.)

Robert Wilson, *The Civil WarS: a tree is best measured when it's down*, 1983.
Photo Jennifer Kotter

THE SCALE AND QUALITY OF OBJECTS IN RELATION TO THE BODY

Relate choice of objects to the scale
and weight of the body

things to pick up in the fingers
to hold in the hand
just possible to carry
fragile things
small but surprisingly heavy
things that can be spilt
soft comfortable things
rigid to hold your weight

bowl of fish   a bundle of pillows
needle and thread   a hammock
a ladder   a peacock

the same thing at two different scales

or much larger than it would normally be

The Great Buddha of Leshan, 71m high, Mount Lingyun, China 8th century

ON LIGHTNESS & WEIGHT

'. . . Your reference to the log makes me want to share some of the
expectations audiences have of female performers, particularly the expectations
of males in an audience. References from males that my work must be
'extremely heavy' or 'extremely light and fragile' because I'm a woman.
Completely ridiculous ideas, because they suppose that any political reference
must be 'heavy' and that any spiritual reference must be fragile and feminine.
The concern of women with spiritual matters has been regarded as
light-weight. The idea of actually carrying around a log was a means of making
this idea ridiculous to an audience – the idea that women performers are either
'heavy' or 'light weight'.

Rose English interviewed by Gillean Chase in *Fuse*, February 1984.

Rose English, *Plato's Chair*, 1983/4
Photo Eric Metcalfe

LET OBJECTS CHANGE YOU, HOW YOU MOVE

CARRY

a large hoop
candle in a draught
tray of marbles
bowl of water in each hand
long pole between two people
a goat

ATTACH

a bale of hay
a lead weight
a weather balloon

WALK ON

feathers
brushwood
a rope bridge

ACTIVATE

a trolley
a net
a ladder

'Making things' took a huge step forwards when I discovered liquid latex which dries to a transparent brown like crêpe soles. It's like copydex, but is better bought from Dunlop in larger quantities. The Bone was the first inflatable I tried to make, so leaky a tractor had to pump air into it all the time to keep it up. My mistake was to use a fabric with a loose weave, as latex is not air proof until thick, and I should have made it with sewn seams. But it looked very good, as I covered the surface with latexed wadding 'teased' out to form a texture of filaments – a very lifelike surface. (Wadding is used to stuff anoraks.)

I had no idea how to make something so big. So I built a bone shape out of branches and straw tied together and then covered it with fabric as one does with papier-mâché, latexed it all, cut it open, removed the contents and sealed it up – mad!

This bone was used for a Forkbeard film called 'The Bonehunter', to protect the grave of a family that has owned the island it is on for thousands of years. A brontosaurus skeleton has been found on the island with the skeleton of an angel in its head – a secret protected by the family, the last member of which buries the snooping paleontologist beneath the bone! A terrific yarn.

Learning from my mistakes on the bone I approached the 'Blue Woman' (see p53) more methodically. I used a fine nylon with a very fine weave, which I latexed on one side before sewing the pieces together, latexing the seams as I went. To get the shape right I made a model of her 9″ high and very carefully cut a paper pattern which totally covered her with a single film of paper. I then layed these pieces on graph paper and scaled them up to 25 times the size – 96 pieces and a hundred metres of cloth – so she would be 15 feet high. The pieces fitted together surprisingly easily. The difficulty with inflatables is the air blows everything out. So if one wants indentations, one has to construct a web of internal strings, stretching across from side to side, pulling the structure to the right shape – while inflated.

The Blue Woman was for a Forkbeard show called 'Myth'. She enveloped the performers in an evil but jovial manner. Everyone thinks she is Maggie Th, but I was just making a vengeful goddess.

Electrolux vacuum cleaners are particularly good inflaters as they have both suck and blow outlets. Two took 4½ minutes to inflate her.

Penny Saunders, *Forkbeard Fantasy*

The Brittonioni Bros, *The Bone Hunter*, 16mm film, 1983
Photo Penny Saunders

BODY AS AN OBJECT

MAKE   dolls   dummies   giant puppets   manikins
objects that refer to the human figure
slides of figures   or parts of figures
human traces   shadows   prints
a heap of people
an identical twin for yourself

WEAR   attachments/extensions to the body
clothes to release you from normal behaviour
impossible clothes
          an enormous pocket
          a thirty foot necklace
clothes to restrict or extend movement
containers to carry or drag about: bags   a box   a trunk

Forkbeard Fantasy

STEVE PAXTON, *Flat*, 1963

In this short piece the performer enters dressed in a suit which he proceeds to take off, hanging the discarded garments on hooks which have been taped to his body. The sequence of events is halted from time to time at unexpected points in the action. The effect is of a series of small surprises – the suit, the undressing, the pauses, and the hooks on the body. These ironic displacements of the familiar are reminiscent of a Magritte painting.

Drawings and notes by Steve Paxton made on request, 1988

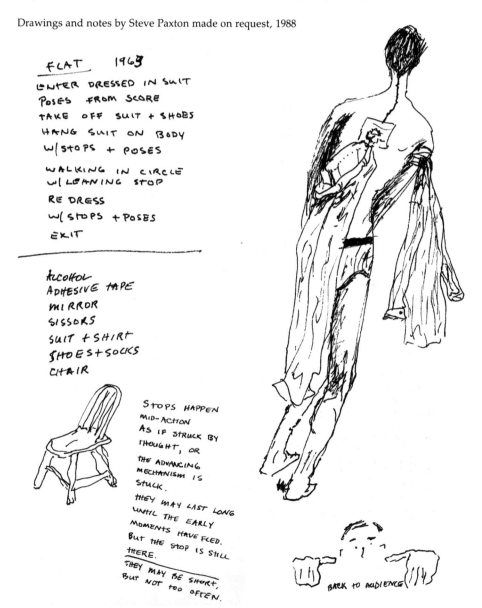

IOU Company, *Wet Maps Dry Seas*, 1978
Photo Daniel Meadows

Trousers and Jacket: the costume motivating the performance. The performers
inhabit the costume exploiting, through a dialogue of movement, the
inferences of parts of a whole – self confronting self, the over-familiarity of
long friendships, the courtesy of new.

Di Davies, 1989

David Ward, *Illuminated Man*, 1981

MAKING OBJECTS FOR IMPROVISATION

We recognise a complex message from a simple sign – a stick can suggest a bird. Because of this, objects made can be very plain. In some ways, the more elaborate something is, the more limited its use and scope for suggestion. Objects acquire interest, not just on their own, but also in combination and in the use to which they are put.

A choice of reality or illusion suggests two quite different strategies for making things. Whereas the traditions of prop making and scene painting are concerned with making one thing look like another (a piece of canvas like a brick wall), in this work it can be just as good to let things be what they are. If you need a brick wall, why not make a real one? Because something is real it does not limit its power of suggestion. A brick wall may become a cliff, a shoulder . . .

Combinations of made and 'found' objects can extend the repertoire. The unexpected use in performance of something that has a known everyday use or significance gives the work an extra dimension –

old pram with attached saucepan
2 boots fixed on top of a wooden box.

Improvisation can apply as much to making things as it does to performing. The making process is one of discovery, in which the precise outcome is unknown at the start. Making proceeds as a dialogue with materials, the maker watching what is emerging and building upon it.

The same image can find many forms, each with its own performance possibilities. It is a matter of finding the form that would be most versatile and evocative –

a horse
the sound of a horse
something used as if it were a horse
a tie-on horse's tail
a Trojan Horse

In the same way, the practicalities of construction almost always call for flexibility of approach –

if you can't get a real horse make one, if you can't make a horse find one someone else has made, if you can't find one draw one, if you can't draw one have an invisible one.

A film loop of a galloping horse is projected as the background to a performance, Sylvia Whitman.

Deborah Thomas, *Hobby Horse*, 1988
Photo Harry Chambers

Hobby Horse involved eighteen performers, twelve of them dressed in huge
sculptural dresses constructed from layers of stiffened, white tissue paper.
Their feet were bandaged onto wooden blocks making them seven feet high.
The figures were set in a landscape of vast hanging sails, 40ft long and 17ft
high, made from tinfoil coloured to appear as if gold leaf and lead. This vision
of moving sculpture had evolved over a period of 2½ years, during which time
the piece was fully performed on three occasions as it expanded to almost
Wagnerian dimensions. From the opening motionless scene, the audience
witnessed a gradual disintegration of a surreal world where two grey
'functional' characters were endlessly employed to mend and reshape, until in
darkness, flames projected onto a final stillness.

Deborah Thomas, 1988.

Photo Kenneth Saunders, 1987

Tim Head, *Present*, 1978
Photo Chris Davies

The projected images cast onto the darkened gallery walls conjure up the
compelling suggestion of a (ghostly) presence, but are merely the pale residue
of an intangible past, forever frozen in time and place, superimposed onto the
gallery's actual space in real time – the continuous 'present'.

Tim Head, 1989

MATERIALS

A floor covered in salt, moss, roses, feathers; a box made of plastic, of wood, of crystal – materials raw or shaped – each has a quality or sensation; we experience each within an intricate combination of cultural convention and physical fact – earth as dirty, earth as a bed.

In one's own personal history, materials often evoke distant memories. The smell of coal or grain or sacking, the taste of a certain type of biscuit, the touch of cork or cotton, may trigger unaccountably strong sensations and feelings emanating from the past.

By placing a performance on a heap of potatoes, or by making a figure in ice, or by wrapping felt around the body, we begin to activate and unloose these associations.

MATERIAL   PROCESSES

burn	balance	weave	nail	squash
dissolve	lean	tangle	tie	fold
freeze	prop	cluster	bind	roll out
crystallise	hang	heap	weld	roll up
filter out	plant	stack	hold	squeeze out
melt	tether	spread	wedge	draw out

Include 'tasks' as performance involving material processes, or use these process descriptions simply as images in movement improvisation or in composing a piece.

Joseph Beuys, *Coyote: I like America and America like me*, 1975
Photo Caroline Tisdall

'Fat and felt were the materials that Beuys made famous and their properties perfectly illustrate his *Theory of Sculpture*: when fat is cold it is solid and can be formed, when it is warm (movement) it flows and has no definite form, so it represents chaotic energy . . .'

Caroline Tisdall on the work of Joseph Beuys,
p14, catalogue for the exhibition, Bits and Pieces, published by the Richard Demarco Gallery, © Caroline Tisdall 1987.

FAT   FELT   SULPHUR   COPPER   IRON

BEESWAX   GOLDLEAF   IODINE

HARE'S BLOOD

HONEY

From: Joseph Beuys, *The Secret Block for a Secret Person in Ireland*, Oxford Museum of Modern Art, 1974.

MAKE A PLACE FOR PERFORMANCE

a place to hide
a place for a meeting
a place for an enormous person

a summer place
a solitary place
a safe place

a place made with 3 sticks
a place with a light
a place made only with sounds

a place unchanged for 2 million years
remnant of a place
a place that comes and goes

a place under a stone
a place to hold in the hand
a place in a suitcase

a precarious place, easily destroyed
a slippery place
an edible place

an island
a world
a labyrinth

several islands   two worlds   lines of communication between

Bow Gamelan Ensemble, *Offshore Rig*, 1987
Photo Jim Harold

Elizabeth Vellacott, *Figures in a Cornfield*, 1953

A PLACE IN MIND

Let the quality of movement be influenced by
the qualities of a place
remembered or imagined

> a hillside
> an endless plane
> a pier
> a table top
> the bottom of a well
> a stone circle
> a glacier
> a phone box

'*Garden* is a landscape. I place a stone here, I place a stone there, here a bush, there I jump this way, that way, taller bushes. I slide along the length of the space, a stream. A frog jumps . . . It's not so much that I make myself look like a stone. It's more that in placing myself I become something that has the presence of a stone. A rock here, over there a rock and by it another and another . . .'

Simone Forti, *Home Base*, Contact Quarterly, Vol V, No 3/4, Spring/Summer 1980, p8.

IOU Theatre, *The House*, 1982
Photo Mike Laye

The House was originally commissioned by Chapter Arts Centre in Cardiff, and a second version was produced for the Almeida Festival in London. In both shows a real house was used as a ready-made setting for ordinary and extraordinary human actions.

The audience was seated in the garden, positioned so that they could see real action in the streets beyond, as well as the dramatic events staged in and around the house. This tension between real and make believe was a strong element in the show.

Each performance began at dusk, with the inhabitants preparing for bed, the audience glimpsing a collage of action through the windows: a woman arguing with her son about homework; a man brushing his teeth; milk bottles being put out. The appearance of an angel on the chimneystack interrupts the prosaic chain of events. He descends to transform the garden, and is joined by two saints carrying beehives. From then on the plot gets very complicated.

Lying on the floor resting, eyes closed.

Imagine walking through a field into a garden, going up to the front door of a solitary house, pushing the door open and going in.

Go through the hall into the living room, then into the kitchen – pull open a drawer. Climb the stairs, go into the bedrooms – open a wardrobe. Go on upstairs to the attic, then go all the way down again and into the cellar. Then leave the house.

As you go through the house imagine what you see there. Who are the occupants? What are they wearing? Do they say anything to you? What furniture and objects do they have around them? . . .

AT ANY POINT AND IN ANY FORM
MOVE INTO THE STORY

At any point leave it
return to resting

Gaby Agis and Company, *Kin*, 1987
Installation by Kate Blacker
Photo Yuka Fujii
© Opium (Arts) Ltd for the world

My collaboration with Gaby arises from a recognition of certain fundamental
parallel concerns in the exploration of our different fields; for example, Gaby's
investigation into the location of movement, articulation and expression
specific to the individual mind and body of each dancer, echoes my
preoccupation with revealing 'place' within an architectural context. Our
collaboration has consisted of a crossing of these parallels. Neither discipline is
in the service of the other, rather two autonomous but sympathetic
investigations meeting and firing off each other.

Kate Blacker, 1989

'Whatever space and time mean, place and occasion mean more. For space in
the image of man is place, and time in the image of man is occasion . . .
Provide that place, articulate the inbetween . . .'

Aaldo Van Eyck, architect, 1959.

PLACE-SPECIFIC EVENTS

Spend time in a chosen setting –

> forest
> beach
> public park
> empty building

Discover what part of it draws your attention

> space under a bench
> between two trees
> a stairway

Occupy this part

Watch   listen
receptive to chance encounters
associations   qualities

G r a d u a l l y

add things to this place
to enhance or make visible its present qualities –

found objects from the setting itself
things brought from elsewhere

Add yourself

Sankai Juku
Photo Setsuo Kato

'Make visible' aspects of a setting that are at present invisible/imperceptible

eg

very slow processes of growth/change

momentary event   as caught in a photograph

historical moment

something too large to be visible . . .
to do with the context within which a place exists

the memories and imaginings of people who use the place every day

Discover the 'invisibles' and bring them to attention through an arrangement
of actions and objects.

WHISPER, THE WAVES, THE WIND
Suzanne Lacy, 1984
Extracts from *Time Will Tell*,
an account by Lucy Lippard
published in the *Village Voice*,
June 1984.

*By the year 2020, one of every five people
in the US will be over 65. This population
will be predominantly female and most of
them will be single. Today women account
for nearly 75 per cent of the aged poor.*

Some walked with a spring in their
step, others crept by on canes. The
audience cheered and wept as the
procession of 150 white-clad women
filed up cliff steps from a sunny La
Jolla beach.

Performances do elicit cheers now
and then, but rarely tears. These were
provoked by the dignity, courage,
and high spirits of women ranging in
age from 60 to 100. The women in
white were participants in California
performance artist Suzanne Lacy's
Whisper, the Waves, the Wind, over a
year in the making, which came to
triumphant fruition on May 19.

Suzanne Lacy,
Whisper, the Waves, the Wind, 1984
Photo/film still Liz Sisco

Whisper, the Waves, the Wind began
with the white-clad women
descending the cliff to become a
tableau vivant when they sat at
white-clothed tables on two small
beaches below a natural amphitheater
of cliffs. As they conversed intensely
with each other, the audience above
'overheard' tapes of their previous
conversations on the same questions
about aging, freedom, death, and the
future. Rocks, surf, sea, and sky
provided a backdrop that was not
only scenic but symbolic. During the
last half hour, the audience
descended to the beaches,
eavesdropped respectfully and then
joined in with questions and ideas of
their own. The women filed back up
the cliff.

Whisper's atmosphere was at once
very real and utterly dreamlike. The
tableau was surrounded not only by
sea and sky but by more mundane
reminders of mortality. Healthy,
tanned, well-dressed and undressed
young bodies contrasted eerily to the
voices whispering around them about
death and decay: 'Aging is sad,
because the flesh shrivels on the
wooden skeleton, and it is not so
pretty.' 'Young people look at me and
see the end of the line. This makes
me angry, very angry.' (An army
helicopter buzzes belligerently
above.) 'The difference between now
and when I was younger is that now
I'm slower climbing mountains.' 'I'm
not afraid of death any more . . . It
would be kind of nice to rest.' (A
Goodyear blimp lumbers by.) 'I'm
preparing to be content if I have to go
to a nursing home.' 'I'd rather be
dead than have to go there.' 'I have
no family. I'm the 13th child and I'm
here by myself. I have no alternative
to a nursing home.' (A formation of
geese wheels above in a graceful
curve.) 'Your children can't face their
loss so they pretend you're not going

to die, and your grandchildren think you'll be around forever.' 'I compare myself to the rest of nature. Everything else wilts.' 'I feel more vocal, more politically free.' 'I want to live because it's so much fun to be alive, so this would be a hell of a time to *die*!'

The whole piece created an extraordinary intimacy. We saw the faces of the performers up close, one by one, as they proceeded down to the beach – women, it seemed, of *all* ages and races (more than a token number of blacks and Asians, including three Cambodian Buddhist nuns), wearing everything imaginable, from formal gowns to ethnic dress to slacks and sandals. When they settled at the tables we began to know their postures and gestures. And when we crowded around the speakers to listen to their disembodied voices, the striking visual image below almost receded into memory because the conversations were so compelling. Each little listening group became a community in itself, smiling tearfully, giggling in recognition. Despite the noise and passers by, I was as drawn *into* this spectacle as I am in the quiet privacy of a dark theater

The elders talked about sex, religion, self-sufficiency, families, illness, and death.

Lacy is an evangelist. She wants 'to enroll people in her vision.' She sees performance art as 'finding the form in non-form, finding the shape in experience.' In the course of telling their stories to each other and to other generations, the elders in *Whisper* provide a historical overview from a rarely reported perspective, educate and entertain others and gain respect and dignity in their 'declining years'. (I've always wondered exactly when these start – maybe at birth.) In *Whisper, the Waves, the Wind*, Lacy succeeds in resurrecting 'an ancient communal art form, the rituals we no longer have. Women are resurrecting it because women's spirituality is in relationship.' When the women in white walked toward us, it was like graduation, a ritual of passage. The light wind blew their skirts and shawls. The tide was coming in . . . not going out. As my mother says, old age is not for sissies.

Rose English and Sally Potter, *Berlin*, 1976
Photo Roger Perry

A four part performance in three different locations.

Part one was at a house in North London
Part two was at the Sobell Centre Ice rink
Part three was at the Olympic Pool, Swiss Cottage Baths
Part four was in the house again

'. . . a house in which we wished to set aside a room to use as a casual
performance venue hopefully untroubled by the expectations attached to
performance presented in art galleries and theatres . . . The other two venues
were arrived at in a number of ways. They were both exciting buildings, both
were associated with sport and both were linked by their physical properties –
the one holding ice, the other water.'

Rose English interviewed by Lynn MacRitchie in Centrefold, April/May 1979.

'The men on the mantelpiece were the chorus; six of them plus a boy. They appeared in the house, on the ice, in the water, and then in the house again, here above the fire. They hold handkerchiefs for their tears, which never come.

The performers included a musician, a writer, a scientist. We fed them but did not pay them money for the shows.'

Sally Potter

Berlin, 1976
Photo Roger Perry

THE FOREST FEAST

'There was a table, in a clearing, at a place where four paths met. This table was slightly raised off the ground by ropes suspended from the trees, so it had an unnatural, unsettling quality, and it was piled with stones and also pieces of bread. The cloth children (stylised humanoid shapes cut from fabric, already stained and partially stuffed in the course of earlier performances) were suspended among the trees, also from ropes. There were chairs set around this table.

'Cameron, Miller and Yeco appeared in the distance, on three of the paths that led to the clearing. Cameron, in the green dress and veil she wore for this entire sequence, advanced on the ground, in a kind of tumbling crawl. Miller, in green and covered with the boxes of various jingling, metallic objects that seemed to signify the apparatuses of patriarchy, advanced on foot, uttering cries. Yeco, who first appeared briefly in a dark suit, removed it to now advance towards the table in white pyjamas, ghost-like. The intense stillness and the slight rustle of the trees gave these entrances a haunted quality.

'The picnic, or imaginary meal, had a tranced, obsessive quality; there was a curious quality of *nostalgia* built in to the sight of the table in the middle of the wood and the chairs, like a picnic in Chekhov, say. There was an enormous distance between the artists, each engaging in rituals of socialisation without any mutual recognition, almost a formal discussion of the spaces between them. Yeco, his head wrapped in a veil, had the air of a risen corpse, a presence, perhaps ominous, perhaps a skeleton at the feast, who Cameron and Miller, Mama and Papa, acknowledged without recognition . . .'

Caldas da Rainha, Portugal August 1977
Shirley Cameron and Roland Miller
extracts from a commentary by Angela Carter

Shirley Cameron and Roland Miller, *The Forest Feast*, 1977
Photo Patricia Leroux

AUDIENCE – HOW THE WORK IS SEEN

Historically established conventions of performance are partly defined by the way in which the work reaches an audience – the circumstances of presentation. These conventions define:

> duration
> setting (eg, indoor/outdoor)
> viewing position (eg, frontal, in the round)
> audience involvement (eg, present throughout or visiting)

For instance, conventions of concert going usually assume a seated audience, a duration of between 1 and 3 hours, and a purpose-made auditorium. But other known forms imply other types of organisation in time and space:

> PROCESSION – performance passes by audience
> EXHIBITION – audience visits an ongoing event
> RITUAL – may take place with or without audience
> FAIR – audience samples parts that interest them

The wide range of common conventions implies further options for performance work including such extremes as:

> performance lasting several days/months
> performance not seen but reported
> performance in a series of spaces with audience led through
> two person ritualistic performance, no audience

Decisions about place and audience affect compositional decisions about duration, viewing position, scale, and materials.

Action that works in a small space, or close to, may not work in a large space or from a distance. A choice of props that looks interesting indoors may look ordinary outdoors.

Welfare State Company, *Lancelot Barabbas Quail*, 1977
Procession through terrace streets in Blackburn, Lancashire.
Puppet maker Maggie Howarth
Photo Daniel Meadows

Alastair MacLennan, *Days and Nights*, 1981, 144 hours non-stop performance at the Acme Gallery, London

It was a 144 hour continuous performance/installation or *actuation* (a term I've coined and pefer) – It was perhaps the first of the really long ones I've done, lasting several days. The Gallery was open 24 hours a day. There was some minimal eating and sleeping (though some later works involve none). The gallery had a shop window front, so that passers-by could see what was inside. This proved useful, as over the 6 days and nights a relationship developed between the regular passers-by and the work (as well as those who came specifically to see it – also with construction workers on the building site opposite). The work involved 'treading the mill' for a 'working week', sometimes clothed, sometimes half clothed, sometimes naked. Some came into the gallery and stood looking. Others sat silently for long periods. Others wanted to engage in discussion. Numerous people kept returning, wanting to communicate.

Alastair MacLennan, 1989

LIGHT AND SPACE

Light shapes what we see, it directs our attention, determining what is noticeable and what is hidden. It offers a simple way of making both large, dramatic changes, and small subtle changes in a performance landscape. The play of light can emphasise form or dissolve shape and solidity, creating ambiguities of depth and scale.

A change in lighting, like a change of key in music, wipes away an image that the eye has become accustomed to and re-presents it with different qualities.

The level, quality and direction of light alters not only the look of a piece, but also scale and timing (eg by isolating detail, or by throwing large shadows of a moving figure).

Henri Cartier Bresson, *Rome 1959*
© Henri Cartier Bresson/Magnum Photos, Inc.

LIGHT AND MOVEMENT

Create a changing series of light landscapes

light close to the floor   in corners   high on ceiling
switched on and off   carried
concealed behind people   furniture   objects

Explore possibilities of action:

in/out/into/coming out of/on the edge of   lighted spaces

What does each setting need?

Watch the impact of each activity on the design of the space in light

Allow the space to change with the action

Large dramatic changes   small subtle ones

vary/balance:

what is foreground   / what is background?

Alternate action and watching

Chris Crickmay in collaboration with Miranda Tufnell, *Installation with Figures*, 1983
Based on an earlier collaboration with Mary Fulkerson

Images were developed from *Facade*, a composition for music and poetry by
William Walton and Edith Sitwell. The installation, built in the café area of a
gallery, suggested the private and turbulent world that often lies behind a
person's social front. The audience looked into a space from the outside
through peepholes. Inside were life-size and miniature figures – falling, lying,
floating, perched upside down – among weather measuring devices,
brushwood and other props. The space was in semi darkness, illuminated by
micro spotlights and hand drawn slides.

A SPACE WITH PROJECTED LIGHT

A room with white walls

A kit of lights/projectors/slides/surfaces/objects

eg   2 projectors
             2 hanging lights with shades on long flexes
             2 wooden chairs
             muslin cloths to hang up
             white panels
             glass slide mounts with materials pressed between
             feathers   moss   hair   leaves . . .

Project slides onto walls in varying combinations
singly   juxtaposed   overlapping

Build settings to intercept/reflect/distort the projected light

eg   2 cloths hanging at angles
             one hanging light near the floor
             a chair in the foreground throwing a large shadow

Explore possibilities of size/position/angle/height

of projected images

Watch the changes in quality of the space

brightness   colour   texture   scale   shape

As a development

Add slides of elements that cannot be present in reality:

         a bird
         a micro-organism
         a busy street
         an explosion
         a past event

Diversify light sources: candle   torches   road-mender's lamp

Miranda Tufnell, *Landlight*, 1989
Photo Dee Conway

dazzling blinding blazing
flashing brilliant
flaring vivid
glinting radiant
sparkling luminous
glistening glittering
steely gleaming
stark shining
sharp lustrous
intense bright
hard strong
clear glowing
white iridescent
pearly golden
misty flushed
cold warm
pale hazy
silvery filtered
grey dappled
watery shady
weak soft
dim subdued
dull mellow
drab dusky
wan coppery
shadowy fading
dingy twinkling
sombre flickering
ghostly faltering
murky guttering
obscure black dark

Rosemary Butcher, *Traces*, 1982
Slide installation by Dieter Pietsch
Photo Matthew White

Lines of light – diagonal, vertical or horizontal – illuminated the bodies of the dancers as they came out from the back to the front of the space and curved round to the back again. Sometimes the lines crept inwards, compressing the space; at other times they moved wide apart. The light rippling across the bodies made them look almost as if they were in water. The dance was a kind of moving geometry influenced by the spacial design of the slides. The slides themselves were keyed into a sound score using a computerised synchronisation system.

Rosemary Butcher, 1989

Paul Burwell, 1987
Photo Polly Eltes

SOUND LANDSCAPES

stillness   sound

dark   silence   distance

action   light

LISTEN

to the sounds of the room
eyes closed   in silence

What is the soundscape of this place/event?
the soundscape of the body
the breath   footfall   heartbeat

Warm up in silence – sounds of the room as a score

Open a door to let the sounds in from outside

Make/map a sound landscape of daily sounds

fridge   clock   wind   rain

Take a walk with a cassette recorder
notice what you are hearing

Find categories of sound
ugly/beautiful   uncomfortable/soothing
Combine and use as score for movement

John Cage . . . 'to compose and perform a quartet for explosive motor, wind, heartbeat and landslide'.

Bow Gamelan Ensemble, *In C and Air*, 1987
Photo Jim Harold

> 'The English excel in dancing and music, for they are active and
> lively: they are vastly fond of great noises that fill the air, such as the
> firing of cannon, drums and the ringing of bells, so that it is common
> for a number of them, when drunk, to go up into some belfrey and
> ring the bells for hours together.'   Paul Henzner, 1605

On finding this quote (some months after being caught by the Glaswegian
Police up a belfry at 02:00 hours) we realised that, far from being part of the
Art Elite, we were in fact operating within the ancestral characteristics of our
race.

> 'Beethoven always sounds to me like the upsetting of bags of nails,
> with here and there an also dropped hammer.'   John Ruskin

For us, I suppose, the converse is true. Not that we mistake the sound of
falling metal objects for Opus No 5, but we find and appreciate and are moved
by such things to the same degree that other people are moved by Beethoven.

> 'This is not music, believe me! I have always flattered myself I know
> something about music – but this is chaos. This is demagogy,
> blasphemy, insanity, madness. It is a perfumed fog shot through with
> lightning.'   Thomas Mann, 1875–1955

'A perfumed fog shot through with lightning' . . . How can we make
something like that? Smoke flares, barbécues and arc welders? Chaos is only
unperceived form . . . Chaos is a concept propounded by rigid hierarchical
societies to abhor self-regulating organisms.

Paul Burwell, 1987

SOUND   SPACES   SOUND   SPACES   SOUND   SPACES
Sylvia Hallet

sound   as thick as a bush
        as thin as a leaf

sound   heavy as blocks of ice
        light as the flight of a bird

chunks of sound which press down on you
press you into the earth

sounds deep as dark water

silence   as a doorway to small sounds

sounds surrounded by silence

        (which is the background, the silence or the sound?)

sounds which have intention: your intention   their intention

        from your inside   as a message to the outside

        which wrap you   cocoon sleep

        intimate like a moth on your cheek

sounds which tumble suddenly

        which ooze their way into consciousness

        with the momentum of a wave   suck and throw

        which pull you from far places

        travel along the sound to its source

sounds   which go with   which go against

SOUND SPACES SOUND SPACES SOUND SPACES

sounds neatly placed
          dropped carefully
          into a pool of silence

sounds scattered from the action of throwing yourself to the wind

sounds which have not yet been uttered
which wait in pregnant silence to be born

sounds of small rooms
sounds of vast spaces

large space – illusion – sound in a small space

sound spaces which co-exist like ghosts
melting across each other

sounds repeating
small circles whirl you through to beyond

find sounds   from inside
                      from outside

pour a sound from one space into another
work with sounds carving holes
shaping soft curves and hard edges

Some sounds need 'framing' to become audible
they need space around them
Some sounds have space in them

All sounds are initiated by movement
substances acting on each other

flick the pages of a book
stir a cup of tea
pick up a plastic bag

Sylvia Hallet

Sound as a holding device
to give the work continuity
a sense of time or timing

Sound as meaning
to bring other contexts into the sound space
of the room
sounds of other places   other times.

A cymbal is struck and thrown into the space. It flies in a great circle
suspended from an invisible thread, hissing through the air.   Yoshi Oida

The sound of walking on gravel moves around the auditorium juxtaposed with
a dance performance.   Cage/Cunningham, *Walk Around Time*, 1968

A dance with tap shoes begins in darkness – only the sound of the
dancing.   Eva Karczag

Sounds of a car chase in darkness followed by light and two dancers stepping
in silence.   Miranda Tufnell and Tim Head

Miranda Tufnell and Dennis Greenwood, *Silver*, 1984
Photo Dee Conway
(hand made slides projected onto figures and objects)

Silver began with a large black ball containing a Sony Walkman (two colanders cushioned in black foam) sent to Dennis and me by composer Annea Lockwood. This provided a moving sound source; we invented a world for it and the sounds that came out of it – a series of slides (made from scratched tinfoil, plaster, string), white sheets, a screen, table and chairs, a bridal veil and an iceberg of transparent plastic, a fish bowl of water and a candle completed the set – a black and white world. We slowly found our way into this world of slides, sounds, etc, creating a series of loosely connected images and events.

QUALITIES OF SILENCE

silence of snowfall

silence of a house

silence of a crowd

silence of a forest

silence of a stranger

an awkward silence

an angry silence

a stunned silence

'My favourite piece is the one we hear all the time if we are quiet'
John Cage

Charlie Hooker, *Skyline Section*, 1987, Banff Center, Alberta
Photo Diana Auguaites

The construction of the piece was formed from a luminous linear drawing of
the skyline of Mt Rundle (which overshadows the Center) stretching the length
of the gallery (approx 70'). Parallel to this were luminous floor markings, above
which were suspended a grid of tuned metal chimes (made from tubular steel
found in the area) and four 'ghetto blasters'. Floor markings (providing a
sound score for the performers, who played hand-held percussion
instruments) were gradually altered by Hooker, and more of the wall drawing
was revealed. The piece lasted 45 minutes, and ended in total darkness with
just the luminous skyline and floor markings visible, the cassette drones and
chimes reaching a peak of noise intensity and then fading away.

Charlie Hooker, 1989

Trevor Wishart, *Tuba Mirum*, 1979
Photo Roger Morton

TUBA MIRUM
Trevor Wishart

The ordinary tuba mute is in itself a strange object, rather like an enormous bung. The special mutes used in this piece include one which has an electrically operated smoke effect hidden in it and also a flashing light. This means that the player can co-ordinate a sudden explosion of smoke which appears to come from inside the tuba with a musical event. The last mute, which can be seen in the photograph, is a cornucopia of very realistic plastic fruit. Hidden within this is a loudspeaker which allows the tuba to project the sound of many tubas and the sounds of animals, birds, and so on; all emerging from the bell of the instrument itself. The use of visual effects and even the simple actions of the tuba player, such as getting the mutes from the box and placing them in the tuba are integrated into a musical theatrical framework.

Trevor Wishart, 1989

4   TOWARDS PERFORMANCE

'I spent a lot of time watching The Grand Union* perform. For hours, I would
see material surface on shaky ground, get nourished, worked, referred to,
developed, and I'd see it begin to strengthen, come into its own, and become
the ground for what happened next. I saw material be given life or death
(which in itself could become the next material), and I learned that there was,
in practice, no inherent hierarchy of material. Every move had equal potential
to unify, clarify, destroy, or transform what was going on. It was not just the
material itself but how and when it was delivered that gave it depth and
power.'

Nancy Stark Smith, *Taking No for an Answer*, Contact Quarterly,
Spring/Summer 1987.

*A Dance Theatre improvisation group including Yvonne Rainer, David
Gordon, Steve Paxton, Trisha Brown, Barbara (Lloyd) Dilley, Nancy (Green)
Lewis, and Douglas Dunn.

Any place, idea, object contains possibilities for performance; an image glimpsed, dreamed, heard – ringing in the mind, a vague sense of 'something there'.

The emergence of a piece depends on how the material is explored and placed. A resonance emerges slowly – significance discovered rather than chosen.

An initial starting image presents itself; its development depends on receptive attention, listening, watching –

a chair

associations surface . . . *sounds of the sea*
an open door
seven people lying face down
figures in bright clothes running between

The early stages of making a performance are those that have been explored so far in this book.

They involve: searching widely, deliberately increasing uncertainty, becoming lost, adding variety and complexity, following wild hunches, attempting the seemingly impossible . . .

Improvisation as a source generates material which, in its complexity and unexpectedness, could never be planned or arrived at by logical means.

The challenge is to carry this through in the more sustained context of a whole performance.

As an image develops it becomes itself a 'landscape' in which particular ingredients belong and others are excluded. Events become more articulated and imagery intensifies.

Developing an idea may involve cycling many times through processes of opening up and paring down material, at each stage deciding what major or minor change will move the work on.

David Medalla and others, *Parables of Friendship*, 1984
Photo Jim Harold

The performance had a narrative structure in prose and poetry which I wrote.
Briefly it tells the story of a white man (a young pilot) whose airplane crashes
in the Pacific and finds himself among a tribe of cannibals who worship the
crocodile. Realising he is about to be sacrificed, the young pilot tries to convert
the tribe to Christianity, hence Western civilisation.

A large stuffed crocodile, painted fluorescent green so that it glowed in the
dark, was gently lowered from the branches of an old oak tree in the grounds
of South Hill Park. The photograph shows the climactic scene of the
performance when the high priest of the tribe, holding a pair of liturgical
candles and stuffed baby crocodile, re-enacts the mystery of Christmas on a hot
midsummer's night. The entire performance which took place at midnight in
the open air of an English park consisted of equal parts of structured sequences
and improvised scenes.

David Medalla, 1989

As the work progresses connections begin to become evident between the various ingredients. A number of independent trails coalesce as a larger territory.

The effect of this clarification is to distinguish essentials from details and to indicate what can be discarded and what needs further development.

The moment of clarification will often come suddenly, in a flash of recognition.

Sometimes this will only occur at a late stage, when material that has been worked on for some time, reformed in a new context, will suddenly gel.

Waiting for a clarifying structure to emerge requires both the confidence and patience to hold out for long enough and the skill to sense the possibility of resolution around the corner.

The structuring task is one of recognising an emergent form rather than imposing one. The material will seem, as it were, to form itself, form arriving via a process of evolution rather than from any preconceived shape. This requires a continual interplay between making and watching.

We refer outwards from the work to the reality of our lives in order to discover structures that reflect the complexity of experience. Imposed forms often filter out this complexity in the interests of order.

Pina Bausch, *Nelkem*, 1982/3

Every known structuring principle offers a potential analogy for forming a piece of work. The stringing of beads, the sedimentation of rocks, the flight of starlings, the packing of a trunk – processes both natural and human – all suggest ways of relating elements in time and space. In terms of a structuring idea it matters little what these elements are.

Living forms are never totally contained. They embody combinations of predictability and chance that make them open to change. Often these structures are not manifested in terms of external shape. Structures may exist internally, as rhythm or inner consistency, easier to perceive than to describe or plan. The way a person walks, their rhythms of speech, their hand writing, are structures of this kind; so too are the structures within improvisation.

In all work there is a balance in the proportion of set (preplanned) to open (improvised) material. An open form raises structural decisions to the level of broad strategy (choice of ingredients, design of the space, general sequence of events). A set form may still leave room for improvisation in certain parts or details.

As the nature and form of the material clarifies it can be refined and edited. This means viewing the work as an outside eye and testing intention against what is actually there. This is a moment for eliminating unnecessary material and selecting certain ideas to investigate more deeply, maintaining a sense of how far the material needs to be pushed in order to yield its potential and to come through to an audience. Weaknesses in a piece of work stem most often from not taking time, not attending closely enough to chosen elements.

The 'visibility' of any element or event
depends on how it is placed.

Continually asking questions:

What can I see/not see?

Is it too long/short/slow/fast?

How does this work with that?

Do I know everything I need to know about this moment?
What if . . .?

Monotony?

Time for a change? a surprise?

What scale of change?

What is missing – from the 'piece' – from the idea?

What prevents the work becoming esoteric – a private language – is an opening of attention to the world in which it takes place; the interlocking realms of personal and public experience.

Part of us is what is around us – our thoughts/perceptions exist within images, associations and assumptions that constitute contemporary culture. We think and 'are thought' by them. They carry dominant attitudes to nature, to the body, to gender, etc, which we may either passively use or actively counter. All work exists in dialogue with other cultural processes and products – with language, with daily roles, rituals, and conventions, with TV, the Press, etc.

Viewing the emerging improvisation with an awareness of these contexts is part of the process of shaping it.

The making of a work is not just a matter of structuring it internally but is also to do with locating it in terms of place and occasion and in its particular historical moment.

Trinbago Carnival Club, Costume for Nottinghill Carnival
Photo Carl Gabriel

Suzanne Lacy, *The Crystal Quilt*, 1987
Photo Peter Latner

A sequel to *Whisper, the Waves, the Wind*, *The Crystal Quilt* was a Mothers' Day
pageant in Minnesota involving 430 women all over the age of 60. The women
conversed at tables forming an enormous quilt-like pattern. The pattern
changed as they simultaneously changed the positions of their hands. The
audience heard pre-recorded conversations similar to those taking place at the
tables.

I never know if a work is 'right' until I see it. But along the way to that moment when, well into the middle of a performance or even near the end, I 'recognise' the image, there are many decisions in which the shape is created. Those decisions are large and small ones regarding appearance, timing, meaning and politics, among others.

Sometimes a decision point comes when, as in the Crystal Quilt, a decision regarding the visual image must be made . . . should we try to find matching chairs and spray paint them black or purchase new ones? The aesthetic, political and financial implications are weighed, generally in collaboration with significant parties, but always – particularly when it comes to aesthetics – I retain the final word. In issues of politics it is different, although I have a sense of my own basic political values that I want to express through the work, I turn the project over to its constituency for guidance in these matters. In the Crystal Quilt one of the most important advisers was Elva Walker, an extremely intelligent and committed advocate for the elderly (herself an older executive and philanthropist). Near the end of our production phase, Elva challenged my intention to have the performers enter the 'stage' of the quilt in procession. She pointed out the inevitable association with funerals that would surround such an entry. Thus we rethought the entire staging of the work so that the performers in black were never seen away from the grounding black of the rug/quilt. They entered four at a time, from the corners and when, at the end of the performance they left, it was decked with hand painted scarves.

The look and the timing, you might say, are the final word, but I judge success on the integration of social and personal meaning into the image. Only when these come together does the work take on the complexity I recognise as art. Creating in this way is a delicate negotiation between inner and outer reality – self and others – to shape a whole. It is very exciting when such moments occur. I don't feel I *create* but rather *recognise* them.

Suzanne Lacy, 1989

In developing an idea the work process may move between some or all of these procedures many times, a changing kaleidoscope of fragments in which parts are added, moved, removed, and the whole is continually transformed.

CHOOSE A REPERTOIRE OF ELEMENTS

number   mix   variety

deliberate excess?   economy?

find initial boundaries of the work

EXPLORE POSSIBILITIES AND QUALITIES OF THE MATERIAL

What action, in what circumstances?
With what mood, intensity, rhythm, smell, sound, connection to other places, times, . . .?

SELECT PARTS OR ASPECTS TO DEVELOP FURTHER

best bits   main bits

ADD/TAKE AWAY ELEMENTS

More/less people, action, sounds, etc
A new ingredient?

EXPLORE RELATIONSHIPS IN TERMS OF TIME

How does one thing relate to/follow another?

in sequence/simultaneous?
separate/synchronised?
in harmony/contrast?

How begin?   How end?   How go from one thing to another?
In what sequence?

Explore possibilities of: fragmentation, repetition, reversal, inversion, change of pace.

THE WORK

EXPLORE SPATIAL RELATIONSHIPS

Groupings of elements – positions/orientations
directions of movement

Relationships in space of different kinds of ingredient –
people, objects, light, sound, . . .

BALANCE THE MATERIAL

more of x?   less of y?

What is dominant, what subsidiary?
A detail becomes a main element?

Adjust relative density between parts:
Too much/too little happening?
How much space/silence/stillness does each part need around it?

Adjust the scale – of gestures, spaces, objects . . .
How large must one thing be relative to others in order to 'read'?

Adjust viewing position(s) – close up/distant, from above/behind?

Find the best duration of the whole and of parts relative to each other:

How much time does an action need in order to become visible?

What parts or aspects of the work should be set/open?

FIND A CONTEXT
(where, how and by whom the material is to be seen)

Location – a tent, a bar, an opera house, a house?

Could the location or type of audience affect the form and content of the work?

Possible relationship to audience and circumstances of viewing – sit and watch,
visit, pass by, join in, see later as photo or video?

I must first sit a little, cooling my arms; that the fatigue may go out of them; because I sit. I do merely listen, watching for a story, which I want to hear; while I sit waiting for it; that it may float into my ear. These are those to which I am listening with all my ears; while I feel that I sit silent. I must wait listening behind me, while I listen along the road; while I feel that my name floats along the road; they (my three names) float along to my place; I will go to sit at it; that I may listening turn backwards (with my ears) to my feet's heels, on which I went; while I feel that a story is the wind. It, the story, is wont to float along to another place. Then our names do pass through those people; while they do not perceive our bodies go along. For our names are those which, floating, reach a different place. The mountains lie between the two different roads. A man's name passes behind the mountains' back; those names with which returning he goes along.

(Statement by Kábbo, African Bushman)

Jerome Rothenberg, *Technicians of the Sacred*, Anchor Books, 1968, © Jerome Rothenberg

Rose English, Sally Potter and Jacky Lansley, *Death and the Maiden*, 1975
Photo Hans Pattiste

SELECTED BIBLIOGRAPHY

Dance

Banes, Sally, *Terpsichore in Sneakers: Post Modern Dance*, Boston, Houghton Mifflin Co. (1980)

Banes, Sally, *Democracy's Body: Judson Dance Theatre 1962–1964*, Anne Arbor Michigan, UMI Research Press (1983)

Briginshaw, Valery and Mike Huxley, *Approaches to New Dance: Analysis of Two Works* in Janet Adshead (ed) *Dance Analysis, Theory and Practice*, Dance Books (1988)

Charlip, Remy, *Now Thyself*, Amsterdam Theatre School (1985)

Cunningham, Merce, *The Dancer and the Dance: Merce Cunningham in Conversation with Jacqueline Lesschaeve*, London, Marion Boyars (1985)

Febre, Michele, (ed) *La Danse au Defi*, Montreal, Parachute (1987)

Forti, Simone, *Handbook in Motion*, Press of Nova Scotia College of Art and Design (1974)

Goren, Beth, *Rapids* (a combination of text and images on Body–Mind Centering) available via *Contact Quarterly* dance journal (1986)

Jowitt, Deborah, *The Dance in Mind: Profiles & Reviews 1976–1983*, Boston, Godene (1985)

Klosty, James (ed), *Merce Cunningham*, New York, Dutton (1975)

Livet, Anne (ed), *Contemporary Dance: an anthology of lectures, interviews and essays with many of the most important contemporary American choreographers, scholars and critics*, New York, Abbeville Press (1978)

McDonagh, Don, *The Complete Guide to Modern Dance*, New York, Doubleday (1976)

Perron, Wendy and Daniel J. Cameron, (eds) *Judson Dance Theatre 1962–1966*, Bennington College (1981)

Rainer, Yvonne, *Work 1961–73*, Press of Nova Scotia College of Art and Design (1974)

Rolland, John, *Inside Motion: An Idiokinetic Basis for Movement Education*, Amsterdam, Rolland String Research Associates, 2nd Edn (1987)

Servos, N. and G. Wright, *Pina Bausch: Wuppertal Dance Theater*, Koln, Ballet Buhnen Verlag (1984)

Steinman, Louise, *The Knowing Body*, Boston and London, Shambhala (1986)

Todd, Mabel E., *The Thinking Body: A Study of the Balancing Forces of Dynamic Man*, New York, Dance Horizons (1959)

Viala, Jean and Nourit Masson-Sekine, *Butoh, Shades of Darkness*, Tokyo, Shufunotomo (1988)

Contact Quarterly dance journal (all issues).
Available from PO Box 603, Northampton, MA 01061, USA.

Dartington Theatre Papers: Barbara Clark, *How to Live in Your Axis, Your Vertical Line*, originally published by Andre Bernard (1968); Mary O'Donnell Fulkerson, *The Language of the Axis* (1976), *The Move to Stillness* (1981–82); Steve Paxton, *Contact Improvisation* (1981–82); Nancy W. Udow, *The Use Of Imagery In Dance Training* (1978)

(Note: It is planned that these and other Dartington Theatre Papers on dance will shortly be available as a single volume, edited by Peter Hulton and Richard Allsopp.)

Art-based performance

Battcock, Gregory and Robert Nickas (eds), *The Art of Performance: A Critical Anthology*, New York, Dutton (1984)

Bronson, A. A. and Peggy Gale (eds), *Performance by Artists*, Toronto, Art Metropole (1979)

Goldberg, RoseLee, *Performance Art: From Futurism to the Present*, London, Thames and Hudson (1988)

Gotz, Adriani, Winfried Konnertz and Karin Thomas, *Joseph Beuys: Life & Works*, Cologne (1973) (Barrons, 1979)

Henri, Adrian, *Environments and Happenings*, Thames and Hudson (1974)

Howell, Anthony, *Elements of Performance Art*, The Ting Theatre of Mistakes (1976)

Kostelanetz, Richard, *The Theatre of Mixed Means: An Introduction To Happenings, Kinetic Environments and Other Mixed Means Performances*, London, Pitman (1970)

Kirby, Michael, *Happenings*, New York, Dutton (1966)

Nuttall, Jeff, *Performance Art Memoirs*, Vols 1 and 2, London, John Calder (1979)

Roth, Moira (ed), *The Amazing Decade: Women and Performance Art in America 1970–1980*, Los Angeles, Astro Artz (1983)

Shattuck, Roger, *The Banquet Years: The Origins of The Avant-Garde in France, 1885 to World War One*, New York, (first published 1955) 2nd edn, Random House/Vintage (1968)

Tisdall, Caroline, *Joseph Beuys*, New York, Thames and Hudson (1979)

Tomkins, Calvin, *The Bride and The Bachelors: Five Masters of The Avant Garde*, New York, Viking Press (1968)

Warr, Tracey (ed), *Live Art Now*, Arts Council of Great Britain pamphlet (1987)

Image-based theatre

Artaud, Antonin, *The Theatre and its Double*, New York, Grove Press (1958)

Barba, Eugenio, *Beyond the Floating Islands*, PAJ Publications (1986)

Blau, Herbert, *Blooded Thought: Occasions of Theatre*, New York, PAJ Publications (1982)

Brecht, Stephan, *The Theatre of Visions: Robert Wilson*, Frankfurt, Suhrkamp (1978)

Coult, Tony and Baz Kershaw (eds), *Engineers of the Imagination: The Welfare State Handbook*, London and New York, Methuen (1983)

Craig, Sandy (ed), *Dreams and Deconstructions: Alternative Theatre in Britain*, London, Amber Lane Press (1980)

Innes, Christopher, *Holy Theatre: Ritual and The Avant Garde*, Cambridge UP (1981)

Johnstone, Keith, *Impro: Improvisation and the Theatre*, London, Eyre/Methuen (1981)

Schechner, R., *Performative Circumstances: From the Avant Garde to Ramlila*, Seagull (1983)